#GetSocialSmart

♡ Katie Lance

#GetSocialSmart

How to Hone Your Social Media Strategy

Katie Lance

ISBN: 1541273311
ISBN 13: 9781541273313

To my husband Paul
You are my rock, my best friend and my biggest fan. I couldn't do what I do without you by my side.

Table of contents

Forward

I met Katie Lance at the first Periscope Summit in September of 2015. Like me, Katie has a passion for all things social media. Every day I help small business owners, entrepreneurs, and brands of all sizes harness the power of social media to build relationships and ultimately grow their businesses. So, when Katie asked me to write the forward for "#GetSocialSmart: How to Hone Your Social Media Strategy," I was extremely honored.

Katie's knowledge and years of experience in social media consulting, speaking engagements, and at press time, the author of over 400 articles covering topics about and related to social media, makes her one of the most credible experts in the field. "#GetSocialSmart: How to Hone Your Social Media Strategy," promises to be a book you reach for time and time again.

Katie brings clarity to something that is often overwhelming to many people - building a social media strategy. Should I use live streaming? What about Snapchat? How does my personal account affect my business? These are just some of the questions going through people's minds when they sit down to build a social media strategy.

Don't worry. It doesn't have to be that way. This book goes into great detail on how to create a social media strategy that works for you. You will learn how to tell the story of what it is like to work with you via social media platforms. **Telling this story is priceless.**

If you are intimidated by any of the social media platforms (and aren't we all at some point?), such as Periscope, Snapchat, Twitter, and Facebook Live, no need to worry. With chapters like "Snapchat for Business", "Live Video, Periscope, Facebook Live, and More!", and "Twitter Tips and Strategies", you will finish this book with the knowledge needed to start your own accounts.

You will find information on the power of visual marketing platforms like Instagram and Pinterest. Visual marketing is a great tool, and I am a firm believer that if these platforms are a match for your business, you must use them. There is power in pictures.

Katie even covers how to develop a content strategy, an editorial calendar, and blogging strategies. If you are thinking, "How in the world am I going to come up with content for all my social media?", you need to read this book. Creating content, and most importantly, quality content, is imperative. You cannot have a successful social media strategy and bring in the sales leads without high-quality content. ""#GetSocialSmart: How to Hone Your Social Media Strategy" gives you the tools you need to conquer your content issues.

You will also learn how to use social media to build relationships and generate new leads and new business. New business is probably the main reason you picked up this book. You want to know how to use the power of social media to increase sales. Isn't that what we all want? Katie does an excellent job of laying out the step by step process of what you need to do to increase your sales. There is even a whole chapter on creating a headline. You can't get more specific than that.

I think Facebook, in particular, holds value for every business out there. In the chapter called "The Biggest Mistakes Business Owners Are Making On Facebook", you learn from other's mistakes on what not to do on Facebook. Have ever wondered how to optimize your personal Facebook account to have the best impact on your business? You can learn that in Chapter 15 "How to Optimize Your Facebook Personal Profile". Katie also dedicates a whole chapter to Facebook Business Pages and Facebook Ads. One of my favorite topics!

Take time to sit down and read this book cover to cover. Include a highlighter or pen and paper. You will need them. The key to a successful social media strategy and to increasing your sales is in this book. Write down your thoughts and takeaways. Study the case studies Katie presents and learn from them. It is through hard work and dedication that we succeed. Luckily, Katie has done a lot of that hard work for you.

There is no reason you can't have a solid and successful social media plan after reading this book. Now get to reading!

Kim Garst
CEO Of Boom Social
International Best Selling Author of "Will The Real You Please Stand Up; Show Up, Be Authentic and Prosper in Social Media", "Success Secrets of the Online Marketing Superstars", and "The Quick and Easy Guide To Branding Your Business".

Introduction

Some of us are lucky enough to do what we love each and every day. When I started my social media consulting firm in 2012, I launched with a bit of blind faith. I wasn't quite sure what was in store for my company or exactly what my business plan would look like. But, I was confident about one thing - that I knew social media and had a lot to offer companies and brands, large and small.

Now, I'm not naïve enough to think I'm the only one passionate about social media. There are thousands of social-media experts, strategists, speakers, authors, and consultants. However, I am a firm believer that each and every one of us comes into this world with a unique set of gifts and talents. For as long as I can remember, I've always loved the art of marketing, branding, sales, and communication. But, it wasn't until social media evolved in 2005 that I really felt like I found my calling.

What makes my company and me different than all the other social media experts out there?

Why is this book different than the other dozen or more on the shelves today?

Well, I know I talk about social media very differently than most people. I feel like there are huge opportunities for brands of all sizes to embrace the personal and the professional side of social media.

There are two sides to the social-media coin, and for most professionals, the professional side is a no-brainer with systems and strategies that you will read about in the book. But, where small-business owners, entrepreneurs, bloggers, and real-estate professionals can really find their stride is in incorporating the personal part of social media (which is often the messy side!).

Social media is where we share our highest of highs and our lowest of lows. It has become our online water cooler; the place we hang out, the place we share our photos of our kids and our pets, the place we laugh and cry and the place we keep in touch with people that mean the most to us.

I'm excited to take you along with me on this journey to talk about how to get smarter with how we think about social media, how we craft a strategy and how we maximize the personal side of social media.

Within this book, you are going to receive insights and read case studies about many of the companies I've had the pleasure of working with over the years.

And numerous, corporate-consulting clients I work with have questions like:

"Which platforms should we use?"
"What are we going to post and when?"
"What is our strategy going to be?"
"How does our strategy fit into our current, overall, marketing-plan?"
"What's the ROI (Return on Investment)?"
"Who will manage our social-media processes?"
"What software do we need?"

And many of these questions probably sound familiar to you too. That's a big factor in why I wrote this book so let's start with the main question…

Why should you use social media?

Social media is a communication opportunity.

In the past, we could use the phone, write a letter, send an e-mail, and visit someone in person. But now, we have this tool that significantly enhances how we keep in touch with people, create relationships and build our business.

Social media has really changed the way that news spreads. Just look at the attacks on Paris in 2015. Within moments after the attack happened, we saw the news flooding our social-media streams. Big brands like Google immediately reacted and offered free, international calls. And Paris Las Vegas dimmed the lights on their local Eiffel Tower.

Remember the 2013 Super Bowl? (I'm a big, 49ers fan so I have to mention this!) That was the game where the lights went out, and it was a huge debacle for many fans, players, advertisers, and more.

But within a few minutes of this happening, Oreo® Cookies took advantage of the situation. They sent the Tweet: "Power out? No problem. You can still dunk in the dark." Brilliant. This is the tweet (heard around the world) that so many marketing and advertising professionals point to when they talk about the power of social media, and the power of being in-the-moment.

In the following pages, I'll share my tips, success stories, experiences, and insights to help you do just that, and more. And while you'll learn some simple, "nuts and bolts" information, the main point of this book is to help you understand and discover how to use social media to meet your specific goals… in the simplest way possible.

Whether you are a real-estate agent, small-business owner, Mom with a blog, large corporation, or someone who just wants to learn more, you'll get the information you need to use social media cost-effectively… without being overwhelmed and without wasting time, money, resources, or experiencing unnecessary stress!

You'll discover your intent for social media, see the benefits of various platforms and learn how to create a strategy for your goals. Plus, you'll have access to actual, success stories so you can see specific tactics in action. It's time to get smart, focus and stop the random acts of social media!

Are you ready?

Chapter 1

●　　●　　●

Don't Be Overwhelmed by Social Media

I have two boys, and for anyone who is a parent these days, you know just how comfortable kids are with technology. Using an iPad or a smartphone is just instinctual to them; they are digital natives. In fact, I still don't think my boys quite understand why the TV doesn't work when they swipe it with their hands!

It's amazing when I think of the period that they're growing up in right now. They'll never know an age when they're completely tied to a desktop or a computer. They have worldwide access at any time with an Internet connection. And this technology is huge.

According to Kissmetrics, 30 billion pieces of content are shared each month on Facebook (https://blog.kissmetrics.com/facebook-statistics) and YouTube has over a billion users (https://www.youtube.com/yt/press/statistics.html). Plus, there is Twitter, Instagram, Snapchat, Pinterest, and dozens of other, social-media sites and applications, with new ones created each day! Yes, it can be completely overwhelming!

But if you just remember a simple fact, it will help you focus… social-media is a communication tool.

Just like you chat on the phone, send an e-mail, write a letter, or talk to someone in person, it's another way to share information. And note that it's not just a way to target Generation X, Generation Y or the Millennials. In fact, one of the fastest growing demographics on Facebook is people over the age of 50.

Today, just about everyone uses social media, no matter what their age. However, you don't want to target everyone. That's why it's essential to be intentional.

Think of social media as a dinner party and not a one-way-street. You create one-on-one relationships where you communicate back and forth. Use social media to find new customers and build relationships over time. Over time, you learn more about each other, form a level of trust and are able to share information to make your relationship flourish. It's not a sprint. It's a marathon. I'm very passionate about helping business owners get more intentional about using social media. If you are tired of spinning your wheels when it comes to social media, wish there were more hours in the day, or have ever asked yourself, "what's the ROI of social media?," then you my friend, are in the right place.

Keep social-media simple. Make it part of your overall, business plan and just start. Here's how…

Chapter 2

● ● ●

Nuts and Bolts - How to Start

I do quite a bit of traveling and meet with many different clients who are in real estate and mortgage, own their own businesses and work in various industries. In a nutshell, I help them figure out how to be more strategic when it comes to their social-media strategy. Because of this, I spend a lot of time flying. And I have a sort of love/hate relationship with United Airlines. (For those of you who fly United, you probably know what I mean!)

A few years ago, I was flying up to Toronto. I flew out of SFO, and everything was fine. But around 15 minutes into the flight, I heard the sound you never want to hear on an airplane… this awful, rumbling sound. And within a minute or two, the pilot announced, "We're terribly sorry, but we're having some slight, engine trouble, and we're going to turn around and land at SFO."

Everyone was a little nervous, including me. But, the pilot and crew were very professional, and we landed without a problem. That part was fine. The challenge happened when we got off the airplane.

Just imagine this. There were around 300 people on this airplane, and we exit onto a gate that didn't expect an airplane to come back. In fact, there were another, two or three hundred passengers waiting for their flight so this small gate area (76 at SFO) grew to a total of about 500 disgruntled United customers within minutes! And to be honest, United just didn't know what to do with us. It was not a good experience by any means. They didn't have enough people. It was very frustrating and very chaotic.

After about six hours at the airport, I still never got onto a flight. Unfortunately, I had to miss my trip to Toronto and go back home. And being the kind of social-media person that I am, I probably did what some of you might do as well. I went onto Twitter and tweeted my frustration about United Airlines. I didn't really expect a response back, and I guess it was no big surprise that they didn't respond. But, I did get a response back from someone else…Virgin America!

They tweeted me back and said, "We're so sorry to hear about your experience. Next time you fly, we hope you fly with us." Needless to say, I was pretty impressed and surprised by the whole thing. It's a story I've probably told hundreds of times. In fact, the irony of this story gets even better. I'm actually writing this very chapter while sitting on a Virgin American flight!

And this whole experience reminds me of the power of social. After all, we're all walking around with these devices and have the Internet in the palm of our hands. If we shop, eat at a restaurant or do something else where we have a really great experience, or a really bad experience, what do we do? We share it on Facebook, Twitter, Yelp, or another platform, right away, wherever we are. And one of the things I've learned is just because you aren't there, doesn't mean the conversation isn't happening. Right? Just because United Airlines didn't tweet me back didn't mean someone else didn't take advantage of that opportunity.

I tell this story because although most us do not have Virgin Airlines' multi-million-dollar budget, there is still a huge opportunity to connect with people, build relationships, and surprise and delight people. And each social-media platform offers different benefits so...

How do you choose which platforms to use?

First of all, you don't have to 'do it all.' I am a big believer that you don't have to be on every social media platform. The key is picking whichever ones are best for you and your business – and go all in with those!

There are numerous venues out there with Facebook, Twitter, Instagram, LinkedIn, YouTube, Pinterest, and Periscope being the top contenders.

I use a variety of these to accomplish my goals, but this will be different for each organization. To find what works best for you, there are a few things to consider.

Determine why you want to use social media. Let's begin by determining your motives for using social media. These are as varied as social-media users themselves, but there are a few, major reasons why business owners and marketers engage in social media including (but not limited to) the following:

1. Create a two-way conversation with their customers and clients;
2. Develop an easy-to-find customer service channel;
3. Respond quickly to customer and client questions;
4. Grow their business by targeting their key audience;
5. Save money with relatively low-cost, compared to traditional, marketing methods;
6. Engage and have fun; and
7. Be where people hang out – regardless of age.

Let's look at a few of the most popular sites to determine which of these options may best serve your purposes.

Facebook

Facebook is still one of the top social-media platforms with more than a billion users. In my book, it's one of the top places to interact on a personal level, build your brand and advertise using Facebook Advertising. I also think there is a huge opportunity for businesses and organizations to build communities and fans through Facebook groups.

LinkedIn

LinkedIn is that professional footprint online. It's the place where people go to find out more about you professionally. If you are wondering where you should start, LinkedIn is my recommendation. Time to dust off that profile and/or company page!

Twitter

Twitter is a great site to expand your sphere and reach people you don't know. It is one of the only platforms that truly operates in real-time so it offers an amazing, broadcast opportunity for businesses to drive traffic back to their sites. And, it also lets you engage with people who are having a conversation about the problem your product or service solves.

Pinterest

Pinterest is a highly aspirational site. It's the place people go to dream about their new home, new baby, upcoming wedding, and more. In fact, people who like Pinterest spend more time on it than any other social-networking sites!

This platform attracts a very strong, female user-base, and it's great as a book-marking site to create a repository of content and drive traffic to your site.

Instagram and Snapchat

Looking to reach the next generation? Gen X, Gen Y and Millennials are all over Instagram and Snapchat. Both are two of the fastest growing platforms!

Video, YouTube and Live Video

If a picture is worth a thousand words, then video, and better yet, live video (such as Facebook Live or Periscope) allow businesses and brands to tell the story of what it feels like to work with them. Video is an extremely powerful medium. And now, with the technology of smartphones, video and live video are not just limited to professional videographers!

How often should you post on social media?

Once you have your social-media profiles set up, it's time to figure out how to use them for maximum effect. Remember, you're looking to build a brand and to stand out from the competition, so a strategy is essential if you want to make the most of your social-media efforts.

With this in mind, let's talk about how often to post on each platform. It's important to remember that not all social-media sites are created equal so you need to adjust your posting-frequency for each one. This way, you can capture your audience without saturating them with content.

Since Facebook is arguably the number-one social media destination with an estimated more than one billion accounts, it may be best to start here.

How often should you post to Facebook?

Thanks to Facebook EdgeRank, not every fan you have will see everything you post. Instead, the more you receive comments, likes and shares, the more widespread your content will become.

To this end, you'll want to post at least three times per week, keeping in mind that daily posting is preferable. Consistency is key.

But don't make the mistake of dropping down to once per week. We've found in working with hundreds of clients, that's low enough to lose audience-connection.

How often should you post to Twitter?

Because this quickly-moving network is far more fast-paced, it needs to be updated more frequently. But, be sure to space out your posts throughout the day so they're not all hitting at once.

I have found that three to five daily tweets are ideal. Keep in mind that given the limit of 140 characters, your posts will be short, but they won't necessarily be short on terrific content. It's easy to do this. Just link to more extensive content in your post.

What about LinkedIn?

When it comes to LinkedIn, you probably won't want to post as frequently.

I recommend 20 monthly posts, which will allow you to be successful in reaching around 50-60 percent of your audience.

That equates to approximately one post per weekday. You might also want to consider joining LinkedIn groups, which are very helpful for making industry connections, establishing yourself as a professional authority and sharing resources.

How often should you post to Pinterest?

Pinterest is a different audience, and thus, a different story. It's considered a high-volume and high-value network. This means you have more frequent posts with smart keywords, eye-catching images and links back to your website. It's also a place where content lives much longer than other platforms – so it can be a great source of referral traffic.

Think three to five-times daily at a minimum, ten-times daily at maximum. Keep the visuals at the top of your mind as this is a very image-driven platform.

Consistency is key!

Ultimately, you need to decide which platform(s) are right for you and your business. There is no magic number regardless of platform. Consistency and having a plan are what matter.

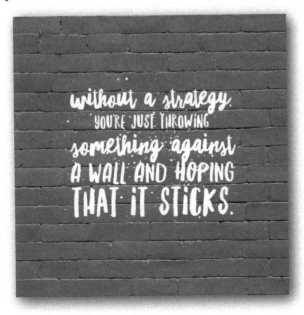

without a strategy, you're just throwing something against a wall and hoping that it sticks.

Also, having the right tools can make a big difference. Using HootSuite, Sprout Social, Buffer, Meet Edgar, or other, social-media platforms can help make this more manageable. But don't forget, your plan-of-attack is the key to success with social media. And, just how do you develop a content strategy plan?

Chapter 3

●　　●　　●

How to Create a Content Strategy

I'd like to start this chapter with an example. Have you seen "The Tonight Show" with Jimmy Fallon? Well, Jimmy Fallon has struck social-media gold as the host.

When Jimmy Fallon made his debut on late-night television, I stayed up to watch. I've been a huge, Fallon fan since he was on "Saturday Night Live" to "Late Night" and am beyond thrilled he is the host of "The Tonight Show."

It's so exciting to see someone from my generation, a true, Gen X-er, grab the reins of one of the oldest and most respected shows in the country and make it new, fun and fresh. The next generation of television.

As someone who advises companies on how to best use social-media to build their brands, watching the brand that Jimmy Fallon has created through social media has been incredible. It is truly the next generation of how we watch TV and interact with celebrities.

Now, Jimmy Fallon is certainly not the first one to tweet his fans or to use a hashtag so what makes his formula work so well and have such devoted fans?

I believe it comes down to five things:

1. **He keeps it real.** Ask most people what they love about Jimmy Fallon, and one of the things they'll say (after they say how hilarious he is) is how real he is. It's not just about being authentic. It's about being humble. Fallon has that rare quality that makes him genuine, relatable and grateful for where he is and how he got there. If there was any doubt, watch the opening clip from his first show. On a personal note, I love how he seems to be just as fired up meeting celebrities as you and I might be.

2. **He surrounds himself with talented people.** Look at who he has around him. He has an amazing tribe of talented people on camera and off. His social-media team did an incredible job building the buzz on Fallon moving to "The Tonight Show." They created a countdown and gave people a sneak peek into the pure buzz that was happening at the studio. They didn't start the buzz with "The Tonight Show." They built excitement for the show for weeks and months before Fallon's premier, and they used social media as their catalyst to drive it.

3. **He cares a ton about his fans.** He talks about his fans all the time. You can tell he is extremely grateful for the support and love he has from his biggest fans. They are always the first ones he thanks, and you can just tell it comes from the heart and a place of humility. He uses social media in a smart way to communicate and crowd source ideas.

4. **His show has a social strategy.** There is a strategic plan in place, and you can tell as you look at the content he and his team have on Instagram, Twitter, Facebook, YouTube, and other platforms. They integrate all platforms and don't just blast the same thing from one platform to another. They respect the audiences in different platforms, and it shows. Part of their social strategy is engaging fans. Imagine if you had a tribe of people who tweeted and blogged about

you. That is the power of social media. It's like word of mouth on steroids.

5. **He blurs the lines between TV and online.** Fallon's team has taken a thoughtful and strategic approach to engage their fans and audience-members, whether it's through their mobile app, on Twitter, on the show's Facebook page, or (especially) on YouTube. The show is also brilliantly creating viral content every night with bits and digital shorts that have a life on TV and then appear on-line too.

Creating a tribe

Fallon has truly created a tribe of loyal followers and fans, and it's partly because of his talent and humor. But, even more so, it's because people like him. He is like your high-school buddy, an old roommate from college, or that guy you used to work with who would always make you laugh.

He's the "Every Man," in a completely charming and charismatic way. And the cherry on top is that he's killing it in social media. As he moves forward in his career, he's bringing millions of new fans along for the ride.

This is true social-media success! So how can you use this example to help tell your brand story in an entertaining and informative way?

Well, if you want long-term success and ROI from your time and effort, it's essential to share good content. Content is the lifeblood of the Internet. Without it, you're left with a virtual, blank slate that doesn't do anything for anyone.

The smart alternative is to create a coherent, content strategy. And, you want it to not only take into account the needs of your business and your clientele, but you also want it to offer a strong, yet flexible, structure for achieving goals through constant evolution.

How to crush your content strategy in 5 steps

Let's break down five things you need to know when creating your content strategy:

1. **Start with the big picture.** Ask yourself about your overarching goals and your company's current, and future, strategy. You need a straightforward roadmap of what you're looking to produce and for whom you're producing it.

   This means you've got to understand your audience. Who are they? What interests them? What are they seeking? Not all people can be painted with the same brush, making it vital to create groups within your audience and strategies to reach all of them.

   It's certainly possible that rather than a single typical-customer, you might have several different-types of frequent clients.

2. **Understand your brand.** How can you create compelling content if you don't know what it's all about?

   Getting a handle on your brand means putting your thoughts down on paper, or pixel, depending on what works best for you. Start by identifying strengths and challenges through an analysis of your competition. How can you differentiate yourself? The answer will help you drive content.

3. **Brainstorm.** Here are several questions that will help guide your inquiry and offer a more coherent picture of what you want to achieve with your content strategy:
   - What type of content catches the mind and imagination of your customers?
   - Who are the most important people to target with content?

- When thinking about who you want to target, how do you want them to connect with your brand?
- What do you want to emphasize in terms of your brand?
- What information does your clientele want?

4. **Delivery of content.** You're ready to begin selecting the ways you're going to deliver your content. This can include any or all of the following channels:
   - Your website;
   - Other sites that you control;
   - Paid channels including sponsorships, pay-per-click search ads and social media promotions;
   - Social media channels (Facebook, Twitter, Instagram, Pinterest, Google+, etc.); and
   - Industry influencers including bloggers and journalists.

5. **Showtime!** Go forth and create your content plan! This may entail an editorial calendar, planner or both. However you tackle the task, make sure that your content schedule flows well and meets your overall goals.

And once you have your content plan in place, you need to create a social-media policy so your team members are all on the same page so here are...

5 ways to tell your story online

Each and every one of us has a story to tell. Our story includes our history, family, passions, and of course, place in our profession.

But too often, our story gets buried on social media.

We say to ourselves, *"nobody cares about the pictures I post from my kid's Little League game,"* or *"why do people post when they are out to dinner?"*

Well, believe it or not, those personal moments help to tell our story and define our personal brand.

Each and every one of us has a personal brand, and it is so much more than what we do for a living.

Telling our stories helps us to connect with others.

So how do we tell our story?

As the saying goes, "a picture is truly worth a thousand words," and this is even more prevalent today in social media. Sharing vivid images and videos are an easy way to connect with people. After all, we connect over photos, especially photos that are real and not stock photos!

And people typically forget what you say or what you write. That's why images and videos become even more important... because they affect how we feel. But where do you start?

How can you tell your story? Here are five of my favorite tips:

1. **Be personal.**
   You must be willing to share and be personal because this is what connects us. Life is no longer black-and-white where we can completely separate our business and personal lives. They are intertwined. And, just like you connect with someone in person over their personality and interests, the same thing happens on social media.

2. **Be real – authenticity is key.**
   Our B.S. meter is at an all-time high. No one likes someone who feels like a fake. Be real and authentic, and people will resonate with that. Don't just like or comment for the sake of liking or commenting. Be genuine!

3. **Share what you love.**
   What are you passionate about? Tech? Travel? Dining? Share things that are of interest to you. This helps to tell your story. Share articles you read that come into your inbox or social stream. If they are of interest to you, they may be of interest to others.

4. **Share moments in your business.**

   Make the most of events that happen every day in your business. This may involve a happy client, fun team BBQ, new hire, and more. All of these moments can be celebrated on social media!

5. **Look at your life as content.**

   What best helps to tell the story of you? Are you a foodie? A parent? A dog person? A wine lover? An outdoors-person? All of these things help to make you personable and relatable and are "content" ideas you can post to your social networks. Our daily moments provide great opportunities for us to tell our story.

Content is about starting a conversation.

When it comes to content, keep it simple, and ask yourself these, top questions:

1. What questions do you get asked repeatedly?
2. What type of people do you like working with the most?
3. Who do you want to attract?

And for blogs and videos, ask:

- Is there an opinion in it?
- Is there a reaction in it?
- Are there opportunities for relationship-building?
- Are you thinking about the long-term?
- Have you looked in your outbox for inspiration?
- What moments or stories are you aware of right now?

Think of content like a muscle. The more you work at it, the stronger it will be!

Now, it's time to get organized…

Create your content strategy grid

Creating a social media strategy is about digging into content, figuring out what content to use, where to get it…all that good stuff. It's a really important piece of your marketing, especially when you think about social and taking your social to the next level.

Content is really king. It's a little bit of a cliché. But it's really true. You know, if you're trying to figure out what you're going to do on Facebook or LinkedIn, or any other social platform, at some point, you're going to say, "What am I supposed to post today?" And if you don't have a strategy, it's a little bit like saying, "What am I going to do today?" Of course, that's not a strategy.

I always like to say, "Content is king." But context is really king. It's one thing to have articles that you're going to tweet out or pictures that you're going to post. But, context and timing is really important, and I feel like it's more important than ever.

For example, if you were to go in your Facebook newsfeed today, you would see so many different things including people posting pictures, articles, videos, and more. And you can see the things that do really well because there are a lot of comments, shares, engagements, and other things that are really relevant. These are the posts that provide valuable content and also catch people at the right time.

Context is important. Are you posting at seven in the morning when it's really not relevant until dinner time?

And it's also important to think of when people are on their devices. When people are on Facebook, half-the-time, they're on their mobile devices so this is something to think about.

Also, how much are you posting? When you're on your mobile device, and you're scrolling through Facebook, and you see a post that says, "See more," are you always willing to click that to open it up? Nope. Me either, so you want to think about the experience of the person who's looking at this, and keep it short and sweet, timely and relevant.

I always like to say, "Without a strategy, you're just throwing something against the wall and hoping it'll stick… just like spaghetti." This is where a content grid comes into play. Some people call it an editorial calendar. Note, you can download your free version of my content grid at http://katielance. com/contentgrid.

This is a really simple way for you to look at the type of content that you want to post relevant to your brand, and then put a plan together for your social-media strategy.

This way, you can think ahead. Instead of living in the moment ("We're at an event, and I'm going to take a picture."), think, "What am I going to post tomorrow?" or "What is my weekend strategy going to look like?" Thinking ahead (and thinking of what you're going to post later this month, or in the months ahead) is very beneficial.

In a content grid, you include topic-ideas. If you really want to get granular, you can write out the entire post and put it in your calendar. But, I personally don't like to do that because I still think that there's a piece of social where you want it to be organic. You want it to be real. And so the way a lot of people use this is to just print it up, put it on a bulletin board, and when they're thinking about their content and what they are going to post in the future, they look at it for inspiration.

A content grid in detail

There are four or five "buckets" of content (or, categories) in a content grid. Here's an example of how you can break it down.

LOCAL REAL ESTATE	NATIONAL REAL ESTATE	LOCAL & COMMUNITY	PERSONAL INTEREST	HOME & DESIGN
Favorite feature of a new listing (think beyond the front of the house)	Link to an article from Inman News	Photo of your favorite restaurant or boutique	Favorite family-friendly places to visit	Before and after photos from staging
Picture of your clients at the closing table	Link to an article from NAR	Best park for kids or dogs	Favorite weekend get-away within two-hours away	Holiday home decorating ideas
Picture of your clients with their set of keys or by their SOLD sign	Link to an article from your local association	Link to an article about upcoming community events	Why you love where you live	Link to an article from HGTV for inspiration
Share a post from your broker or franchise	Link to an article from HousingWire.com	Link to one of your Pinterest boards highlighting different neighborhoods	Your favorite local sports team	Link to one of your Pinterest boards highlighting different rooms or design styles
Monday market update - a one-minute video you create	Throwback Thursday #TBT - home prices then and now	Link to one of your favorite local bloggers	Your charity of choice	Photo of one of your client's homes after they move in
Photo or video of a past client with their story of how you helped them	Link to an article from the New York Times on housing	Best place to get a cup of coffee or a glass of wine	Behind-the-scenes: why you love what you do	Photos of your favorite home details
Graphic featuring a review you received online	Photos from real estate events you attend	Important school dates and info - link to the school sites	Photos of your team and/or your office	De-cluttering or home improvement tips

Bucket 1

As an example for a real-estate company, the first bucket is Local Real Estate. Here, you insert things like favorite-feature of a listing. I always say, "Don't just talk about listings on social media, but get creative." You know, maybe it's a beautiful photo of a view. Maybe it's the really cool, kitchen knobs on the cabinets. Perhaps, you can add something about the local neighborhood or community, market stats, home-improvement tips, and more.

Bucket 2

The second piece shows National Real Estate. While it's important to post local information in the real-estate world, there's also a great opportunity to post things that are national, like articles from The Wall Street Journal, Forbes, The New York Times, or Inman News that talk about housing, real estate or what's going on in the economy.

You may also want to compare home prices. In the past, Zillow has does this every Tuesday with "Taste Test Tuesday" on Facebook. Here, they'll put up two, beautiful homes at the same price-point, and it will say, which one do you like better? It's a fun way to talk about a house, and they include a link to the listing underneath.

You have a great opportunity to talk about homes you've sold, or homes that are on the market, in a really creative way.

Bucket 3

The third bucket is Local and Community. This is a really important piece of the whole strategy. When discussing real estate, it's so much more than the house, building, condo, or whatever it is. It's…

What does it feel like to live in that community?
How close is it to downtown?
What are the schools like?

And all of that local information is key, for example the best place to get a burger, the best place to get a cup of coffee, and more. If you can infuse some of that local content and information, it really works.

A few years ago, I was in Boston for an event, and one of my good, agent friends was driving me around. We had three hours, and he was showing me where he lives in Boston and telling me all about the various buildings and founders, and more, and I loved it. And I told him, "You know what? I love real-estate agents because you know all these things." And you might think, "what's the big deal?" But, all those little pieces of content about your neighborhood are awesome for social media.

Bucket 4

Your social media cannot just be about business. When you look at your strategy for what you're going to post to Facebook, Twitter, LinkedIn, or any, other social-media-strategy, there's got to be a personal piece to it. And, it's going to be different for all of you. Some of you might be more comfortable sharing more personal things than others. But it's important to find something personal that you're comfortable connecting with and sharing.

People connect with things that are personal to you. Whether you're a mom, grandmother, dog person, a foodie, love to cook, etc.., whatever those things are, you may think they are not that big of a deal. But, those things that are important to you are what that people use to connect with you and connect with other people. That's why it's essential to include a few, personal items in your content grid.

Bucket 5

The final bucket for real estate is home and design. Real estate for many people is very aspirational; it's the American Dream! By incorporating design ideas, before-and-after photos, and inspiration from sites like HGTV or other, home-design sites, you help to paint the picture for your potential clients. Plus, you provide really fun and engaging content.

Make the grid simple and your own

While I discuss the real-estate industry as an example, edit your content grid, create it and make it your own based on your personal brand. To make it easy, you can create your content grid using Google Docs, Google Drive or the Evernote app. This way, anyone helping you with your social media can access the information online, and you can see the changes people make in real-time. You can also go old-school with a simple, Excel spreadsheet or pen and paper.

Just be sure to include your buckets of content, or categories. While my sample shows five categories, you may have more, including topic ideas. Your categories should be four or five things that are relevant to your brand.

Here are some examples of various businesses and what their buckets (or topics) may look like:

- Winery: wine trivia, varietals available, wine club, events, giving back to our community
- Photography studio: tips and tricks, photo ideas, our customers, behind-the-scenes
- Mommy blogger: my favorite products, tips and tools, lifestyle tips, favorite gadgets, personal
- Event coordinator: event spaces and places, do's and don'ts, tips and tricks, looking your best, locations
- Insurance salesperson: best practices, real-life examples, life, home, auto, do's and don'ts
- Social media consultant: do's and don'ts, tips for platforms, live video, best practices, mobile

And to find topic ideas, just think about all of the things that you talk about most often.

What are things that people ask you?

What emails are you sending out?

If you find that you're frequently giving some of that same information in your emails, that will make good content. I always say, "Look in your Sent Box." A lot of times, what you're sending out in your Sent box is great information that you can post to your social networks.

For me personally, if I get asked a question more than once, I make a note of it. And, many times, this becomes a great source of content – whether that is a blog post, video, graphic, or live video!

And in addition to topic ideas, you'll also want to include a list of go-to sources. After all, you need to figure out where you're going to get your content.

When I first dove into social-media strategy, figuring out what I was going to do was a big piece of it. One of the first jobs I had that required social media was for a real-estate company in 2005, when social media was in its infancy. And I remember thinking, "OK, I need to get a system together if we're going to do this Facebook thing and if we're going to do this blog thing."

Then, one of the first things we did was ask, "What are going to be our go-to sources? If I need to post content every day to Facebook, Twitter and LinkedIn, and we're going to use this to build business for the brokerage, how are we going to make this work?"

And so I brainstormed a list of five or seven sources, websites, that I would go to every morning and take 10 minutes to look for interesting articles that I would send out. These were things like information from the local Chamber of Commerce, articles from The Wall Street Journal, and different websites that I found valuable.

To help you get started, here are a few ideas in terms of go-to sites. And they will be different depending on what market you are in.

- **Your local, downtown association, if you have a local city-website**
  Usually, most cities have a city website, and then there's some sort of downtown association, or some other city-site, associated with that. That's always a great site because it's local content.
- **Chamber of Commerce or Patch.com**
  In addition to your local Chamber of Commerce site, check to see if your city has a Patch.com site. This is a good site because there

are local bloggers that contribute to Patch, and it's really fantastic for finding articles relevant to your area.

- **Local blogs**

 In San Francisco, there's Seven by Seven. In New York, there's Curbed. Check for local blogs for some great information.

- **School-district sites**

 The sites that provide school information are a must-have. Is it a snow day? Is it a teacher work-day? You might think, "Well, that has nothing to do with real estate or your business," but that's ok. This is because a big piece of your content strategy may have to do with positioning yourself as a local expert, knowing the community and being a trusted resource.

Types of content

There are all different kinds of content you can curate including…

Article links

Linking to articles is a low-hanging fruit. It's one of the easiest pieces of content. You simply find a great article, and you click the Facebook share button or the Tweet button, and you share it out on your social networks.

Now, when your share a link like this, don't just share the link. Put a little commentary in it. For example, if I saw an interesting article from Inman News, I would share that on Facebook and say, "Hey, just read this great article from Inman about the housing market. What do you think?"

Blog content

If you're a blogger, how often are you going to be creating blog-content, and how often does that fit into your social strategy? If you're creating content, a blog or a video, it's probably not going to just get posted once. You might post it once to Facebook on a Friday and then Tweet it out Saturday morning, Sunday afternoon, and Monday morning. Because of this, it's important to think through your content process.

Photos

Photos, I think, are one of the easiest types of content because we're all walking around with smart phones, iPhones, Androids, and more.

If you're like me, I've got a bunch of photo apps on my phone. And photos are one of the best sources of content. If you scroll down your Facebook newsfeed, that's what you see… photos.

30 PHOTOS IN 30 DAYS

- Imagine if you drove around your local community and took 30 photos; a photo of the downtown main street, the historic building, the neighborhood park, your favorite coffee-shop and pizza place, and more.
- Then, with these 30 photos you can use an app or two to enhance them to look fun and interesting.
- Now, you have 30 days' worth of content that you can post to your social media channels. It's really as simple as that to create your own content in terms of photos!

And one of the things that's really fun to see is more and more agents using their own photos on their website and blog. I'm seeing far less of the stock photos (You know what I mean… like the standard "shaking the hand," photo). If you can use your own, "real" photos, that is really what connects with people.

Videos

There are so many great video apps where you can create quick and short videos. Of course, you may have professional videos done for your business, real-estate listings, and more. And these can be pieces of content you're posting on social, but also try quick videos.

I know some real-estate agents who are using Instagram video. They take a quick video and do a sneak-peek into a home where all you see is the door opening, and then, you see or hear something like, "I'm so excited to present this new house," or "This is coming soon on the market." It gives you a sneak-peek into something that they're working on, a client that they're working with, or a quick testimonial of, "Hey, it was so great to work with so and so. I can't say enough great things about them." Videos can help you share a unique message and provide a great, content source.

Questions

By asking questions on your social networks, especially Facebook, you can start a conversation. For example, you can ask, "Have you lived in your house for five or more years?" This is a great question for people in real-estate because you'll receive a lot of comments and replies. Some people will say, "No, but I'm looking to buy a home." Then you can say, "Well, call me." Right?

Some other questions are:

What's the number one thing you love about your city?
What's the number one thing you love about San Francisco, New York City, Seattle, or somewhere else?

Are you going to the holiday-event downtown this weekend?
How old were you when you bought your first house?

These are just simple questions, but the whole point is to get people engaged. You're not just posting something out there to post something and be boring. Be interesting! Questions are really relevant to your brand, your neighborhood and what you're doing. Plus, they can be a great source of content, as long as they are simple and not too complicated.

Tips for curating good content

With that, I have a few ideas for curating really good content.

Flipboard

This is a great app for curating content based on subjects like real estate, Denver, housing, etc. where you see specific, news sources. You can easily pull stories into Flipboard from The New York Times, The Wall Street Journal, and other, news sources. Then, you just flip through the stories, find interesting articles and share them.

You can also pull in your Facebook and Twitter feeds, which is really interesting. I always seem to find things that I've never seen before on Facebook, and I can reshare those and post those out to my network via this app.

Houzz

Another one of my favorite sites for content is a site called Houzz which has some wonderful ideas for decorating different rooms. By clicking on a tag, you can buy the various objects showcased in that room. But, what I like about it for social is it's like eye-candy for people.

You think about why people love watching all those HDTV shows, and it's because of beautiful photos like those shown on this app. And they are fun to share… "Hey! Do you like this kitchen or do you like this kitchen?" It's a great site for finding interesting content and things that are really going to resonate with people in your networks.

Google alerts

Google Alerts is a good source for content too. If you've never used it, you just go to Google and type in "Google Alerts." It will take you right to it. And Google Alerts is nice because you can put in cities, schools, communities, the name of your business, the competition, and whatever else you want to monitor.

I know for myself, when I was curating content for real-estate brokers that I was working for, we would have different Google Alerts set up for four or five different neighborhoods, schools and community activities. Then, any time that word is mentioned on the Web, you get an email letting you know with a link to the story.

It delivers right to your inbox, and then you instantly have a list of articles relevant to your business that you can share via your social networks.

Twitter

Regardless of whether or not you are on Twitter personally, you can really leverage it for content. One of the things I love that I've been able to do on Twitter is create a local-news list. And this is something any of you can do by going to twitter.com/lists.

I did this recently to create a list of local content and news into my area. I went into Twitter, searched for local news-stations, newspapers, blogs, and other resources I new about, and came up with a list of about 28 sources. Then, I added these to a list which I can reference any time on

Twitter to see if there's anything interesting and relevant to retweet out to my followers.

And even if you're not on Twitter, you can find great content relevant to your audience, click on the stories and share them via Facebook, LinkedIn, Twitter, and more… quickly and easily.

Images

I mentioned this previously, but images are one of the best pieces of content and can really make a big difference in your social-media activities and number of shares.

And what type of photos are being shared? These can be images of the community, neighborhood, views, downtown area, coffee houses, pizza places, happy clients, buildings, office pets, and more. Think beyond the standard photo. You can use professional photos, but remember, you can also use an Instagram photo or something where you're just showcasing the detail of something.

Over is a great app for writing text and placing it over a photo. I also like Camera Plus and WordSwag, but there are many apps out there to choose from.

Video apps

There are some apps out there that will help you create and share video content. For example, Videolicious and Animoto are fun and make videos really simple.

The key is not to get intimidated by video. Instead of worrying about what to say, how you look, what to edit, and more, just capture a moment, a really simple moment. This could include time with a client, features of a home or business, someone using your product and more. For example, try doing…

Community videos

It doesn't have to be a full-fledged video. It could be three things that you love best about your community where you take just five seconds, and you use one of the apps. It stitches it all together for you.

You pick some music, and it's beautiful and easy. Other ideas are to do short and sweet testimonial-videos and sneak-peek videos where you show a brief snippet of a home, business, product, service, or something else.

Now that you have some ideas on how to move forward, here are my favorite video tips…

Sound and script

No one likes how they sound on video so you just have to get over that. I always like to say, "Be organized, and not scripted." And if you're the kind of person who needs to be scripted, then maybe that works for you.

When I do videos, I just like to know what I'm going to say and create bullet-points. I know how I'm going to start, and I know how I'm going to end. I might have a few bullet points and then I go. That makes it a lot more natural.

Have a beginning, middle and end

The beginning can be something like, "Hi. I'm Katie Lance with Katie Lance Consulting, and today, I want to share with you my three, favorite reasons why I love New York City."

Then, you give the three reasons and end it with your call-to-action. Don't just say goodbye. Instead, tell viewers what you want them to do (whether it's to visit your website, call send an email, or something else). For example, "Thanks so much. If you have any other questions, feel free to contact me. I'm at KatieLance.com."

Pinterest

Pinterest is one of the fastest growing networks. The number one thing that's talked about on Pinterest is the word "home." And, what we found is that people who are on Pinterest are spending a lot of time there – way more than any, other social-networks.

Pinterest is interesting because of all the different things that you can pin. It's kind of like a scrapbook and pin boards from years ago. All of these pin boards provide great pieces of content so if you're thinking, "Ok, again, what am I going to post, and what makes sense?" this is a great place to start.

Instagram

It's the same thing with Instagram. When you're out at a party, a store, working with a client, and more, and there's an opportunity, snap a photo. Then, you can tell a story or encapsulate something that has to do with your brand via Instagram using Instagram photos, video Instagram Stories and/or Instagram Live!

Now with Instagram, I post photos of my sons, pictures of wine (which I like a lot!), people at events, and more. Just like any other piece of social, you've got to get personal. But again, it's whatever you're comfortable posting. (I certainly don't share every single photo of my kids. It may seem that way, but I don't!)

Look at your life as content

It can be easy to get overwhelmed about what you're going to post. I think one of the best things that you can do is just look at your life as content.

What are you going to post to Facebook, Twitter and LinkedIn?

Well, what are things during your day that you tell a story about? Here's a few scenarios:

- You're at an office meeting. Who can you highlight at that office meeting? You've got 50 people in a room. Who can you take a picture of right there, highlight them and put them on your Facebook page that afternoon?
- Who has a success story? They just closed a big deal, right? And they're so happy because they just worked with the most amazing couple, and they just relocated and they have two young kids. Wow, that's something meaningful you can share!
- Or you are at a conference, and you just met the most amazing people, or listened to a great speaker. What a great opportunity to send a tweet praising the speaker or post a photo to Instagram from the event.

Look at your life as content, and what are those opportunities to share, whether it's personal or professional!

Content is everywhere. You just need to be aware of it, capture it and get ready to share it via an organized content strategy!

Now, how can you repurpose that content...

Chapter 4

How to Repurpose Content Across Multiple Platforms

Many people often ask me if they can just have content, put it somewhere and then push a button for it to go everywhere. And, you actually can. However, I'm not going to tell you how because I really recommend you go against that. And the reason why is, sure, you can take your tweets and push them to Facebook, and you can push every Instagram photo to Tumblr, and do this and that, and that certainly would save you time.

But, the problem with this is that every social-network has its own nuances and kind of etiquette. And I'm sure some of you who have seen your friends pushing all their tweets to Facebook, right?

I have a few of those friends. And I've gently reminded them that it doesn't quite work because a tweet doesn't really translate to Facebook. The content may be ok, but with Twitter, you've got the "@" sign and the hash tags. It just doesn't work because Facebook is different. I always say, "Don't re-invent the wheel." If you've got a great blog-post or a video you created, don't just post it in one place. You can post it to all your networks. But how you talk about it is going to be a little bit different for each venue.

If I do a blog post, I may post it to Twitter and keep it short and sweet. I'll put the topic of the article, the link and a possible hash tag or two in the tweet. I might tweet that article out four or five times over the course of four or five days. But then, I'll also take that article and post it on Facebook with a few sentences. I'll say, "I was really inspired to write this blog post because….. What do you think?" And then, I'll also take that blog post and place it on LinkedIn. Or, I might put it on Instagram if it's a photo. I'm a big believer in not re-inventing the wheel but just being really cognizant that every network has its own landscape and language.

Did you know this about Facebook?

In addition to repurposing where you post your blog posts, you can also do something unique with Facebook to extend the life of your posts. Facebook post has its own, unique URL. This means that when you post something to Facebook, you can actually promote that post somewhere else. For example, instead of saying, "Check out our Facebook page," you can specifically say, "Check out this photo."

To find the unique link for a Facebook post, you just click the time and date stamp. Then, it will open in a separate window and you'll be able to see the really long URL at the top of the page. This is the unique URL that you can then tweet out, publish on LinkedIn, put it on Instagram, or post it elsewhere to promote that specific post. It's the same image, but it translates a little bit differently across each platform.

Postagram

So Postagram is a really fun app where you take an Instagram photo and create a physical postcard that you can actually send out via snail mail. It's really beautiful and looks professional.

You simply put in an address and a nice, personal note. Then, you can easily take what you're doing online with those online Instagram photos, and send a thank you card (or note that you're thinking of somebody) to the offline world.

StickyGram

Another fun kind is StickyGram. It provides magnets made out of Instagram photos. There are many possibilities with this. As I always like to say with social, "Think outside the box." What if you are in real estate and take eight or ten photos of a client in their house (family photos telling the story of them moving in their house, maybe popping the bottle of champagne, etc.) You can take those photos, order the magnets and then send them as a nice surprise. Your clients will appreciate your kind and unique gesture, and the magnet will be on their refrigerator as a reminder of that moment, who they worked with and the whole experience.

Extend the life of a post.

A typical Facebook post is active for about three hours. This means that Facebook pushes your post to friends and people who like your posts, and after around three or four hours, it kind of goes down to the bottom of the pile. To extend the life of the post, grab the unique link for that post that I mentioned earlier. Then, tweet out the link, post it to LinkedIn, send it out instead of an e-mail, and more.

Another little secret that no one seems to talk about is that it's not what you say, it's how you say it. And I see this all the time. I see people who have the best of intentions. They come to a class or they hear a webinar and they're like, "Alright, I'm going to do this. I've got the content grid. I'm going to post content 10 minutes a day. I've got it, Katie." And then they go on Facebook, but they're doing it wrong.

You might go, "What's the big deal?" But if you're going to spend the time to have a strategy and post to Facebook, Twitter and your social networks, a lot of little things make a big difference. Review how you write your posts so that they are interesting to others. This is important, and most people don't even talk about this factor when it comes to social media.

How to perfect your post for every social media platform

Not all social platforms were created equal. Here's how it breaks down and where we've seen the most success with our clients and with our own company:

Blogs:

- Create an engaging title that grabs a reader's attention. It's best to keep it under 70 characters.
- Feature any keywords in your first paragraph. Make it clear what readers can expect from the post.

- Make your post pop with relevant images.
- Summarize your post with a call-to-action.

YouTube:

- Create a catch title to hook viewers from the beginning.
- Use that catchy title when uploading (rather than something generic)
- Help people find your video with a smart description that includes links to your website and other, social channels.
- Include tags to help your video appear in searches.

Facebook:

- Keep it positive. Positivity breeds engagement.
- Provide information and a link so readers will want to click... and they can.
- Include images.
- Make it mobile-friendly. More people are using smaller devices.
- Engage with users through conversational dialogue.
- Be available to respond.

Twitter:

- Offer a clear call-to-action to get readers thinking in terms of what you want them to do.
- Don't forget punctuation. It's important!
- Shorten URLs. Bit.ly is perfect for this.
- Engage viewers and drive retweets by using questions, facts and figures.
- Prompt engagement through mentions.

- Retweet relevant content for readers.
- Images and videos heighten engagement.
- Ensure that your punctuation is perfect.

Pinterest:

- Share without images of human faces. These get shared 23 times more often than their face-full counterparts.
- Use a compelling background that takes up less than 40 percent of your image.
- Get three times the number of likes and repins with multiple-color images. Red or orange images are particularly popular.
- Increase repins by four times using images with 50 percent color-saturation. Black-and-white images don't do as well.
- Incorporate vertical images instead of horizontal ones. Go for a ratio of 2:3 or 4:5 for the best results.

How to repurpose your blog posts or live streams

Periscope broadcasts or Facebook Live

I live stream just about every day, but I don't repurpose every, single live stream. When I first jumped on Periscope, I was broadcasting two to three times per day and getting a little burned out with having to come up with content.

With this in mind, I've changed my strategy a bit this year. I decided to do one, big scope or a more in-depth Facebook Live once or twice a week. This is the #GetSocialSmart where I dive a bit deeper into social-media strategy. Generally, this is the live video that I really focus on repurposing, specifically for my blog.

To do this, I save the scope by saving it to YouTube and then embed it into the blog post. I can also do this with a Facebook Live; I can embed the actual Facebook Live into a blog post or take the actual video and upload it to YouTube to embed.

Another value of doing this is that I do a lot of promotion around my weekly show through Facebook, Twitter, Instagram, LinkedIn, and Google Plus. I believe the art of repurposing content is not just to create content and blast it everywhere, but rather, it's creating content and seeing how far you can stretch it over the course of time. That's when you really win the game; when you can take a piece of content and stretch it out over 7 days, 14 days, 28 days, 6 months later, etc.

I also broadcast live into our #GetSocialSmart Academy Facebook Group once a week or so. Broadcasting directly in a group allows me to connect with our Academy members, provide unique content, answer questions and build community.

Blog posts

With a few of my blog posts, especially the really hearty-posts or guides that I create, I like to slice and dice them over time and see how far I can stretch them. A great example of this is my Snapchat for Newbies post on my blog (http://www.katielance.com/snapchat/). With this particular post, I created the blog post, and then about a month later, I created a SlideShare of the post and embedded that into the blog. I'm a huge fan of SlideShare, and it's a fantastic tool for repurposing content. SlideShare is also owned by LinkedIn so it connects easily to LinkedIn, providing another, great benefit.

Then, another month or so later. I went into my SlideShare and created a video. I uploaded this video to YouTube as well as embedded it into the blog. Again, by doing this, I was able to add new life to my original post. Finally,

I created a graphic for Pinterest (using Canva.com) and embedded that into the post.

Now, the reason I bring up blog posts is because I believe the heart of repurposing content really starts and ends with your website. If you really want to build your brand, it's important that your content lives on a platform that you own – your website. Generally, that will be your website's blog section.

Here's an example of how we think about repurposing content:

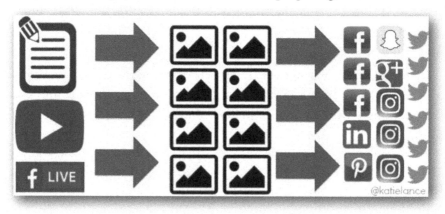

Promoting your content

If you're feeling like you're spinning your wheels when it comes to content creation, I invite you to look at your promotion systems. When it comes to promoting content, I always say you can't wait for people to come to you. You need to be putting yourself out there, repeatedly.

Here is a helpful checklist for promoting your blog posts:

- One of the first things I do when I create a new piece of content is think, "Who are the two or three people I could send this to first?"

Don't forget there's magic in the one-to-one. I know that may sound a little corny, but when you can reach out to people and tell them you thought of them when creating the content, it can go a long, long way.

- Another key, promotional effort I do is send content out through a dedicated email. Email marketing has been huge for growing my business. Not only do I send one-off emails, but I also deliver a regular, weekly newsletter full of tips, resources and helpful links - like my most current blog posts!

- Other ways I promote content is putting a link out on Facebook (I like to post organically to Facebook and don't use any, third-party service). I will generally boost these posts for a small amount of money for four to five days. I also use Hootsuite and Edgar to schedule out the content through Twitter several times over the first, few days and then continue to auto-drip out over the course of time.

- Finally, I'll also post to LinkedIn and Google Plus, and create images for Instagram and Pinterest

Now that you have a better understanding of repurposing content, now it's time to learn how to write better posts. Let's start with creating good headlines that build buzz...

Chapter 5

• • •

How to Create an Awesome Headline

They say there's never a second chance to make a first impression, and this is especially true for your posts. When you're writing a headline, you're not just putting together a series of words – you're enticing your audience to read what you have to say.

Generally speaking, 80 percent of people will read headlines, only 20 percent will go on to read the rest of what you have to say. Hook them in the beginning, and you have them through the end. A great headline is the way to open up a productive dialogue with the people you want to reach most so here are some tips...

1. Make it powerful.

You want your headline to be powerful enough to get your first sentence read. Toward that end, it pays to focus on crafting a headline that will capture your customers and make them *want* to read the rest.

Strong, powerful language keeps people reading.

2. Make it memorable.

People just don't remember calls-to-action that are dull, bland or boring, and can you blame them? Differentiate yourself from the competition by taking the time to come up with a unique message that will stick with your audience.

Words, words, words. Choose carefully.

3. Specificity is your friend.

You don't have to bore down into every detail that your customer needs to know. What you're trying to do is get them to read on so that they can learn more. However, you do need to provide enough, relevant details for them to understand that they *need* to read on because what you're talking about applies to them.

Specifics are good, but don't overstuff your headline with them.

4. Urgency is key.

If you're looking to get your message across, make sure that your headlines convey some sort of carrot for your customer. If they can't understand the benefits, your chances of hooking them sinks dramatically.

Your call-to-action must spur some sort of emotion in your audience.

5. Is it useful?

Finally, your headline must be useful to the person who is reading it. You want to let them know that there's something in it for them and that continuing to read on can make a positive difference in their lives. Don't hold back here. Get them hook, line and sinker.

6. Focus on your headlines helping or solving a problem.

How many times have you Googled, "How do I..."? If you can create headlines (and content) based on the problem your product or service may solve, then you are on the right track.

7. Use positive or negative superlatives.

What's a superlative? It's an adverb or adjective used that is greater than any, other possible degree of the given descriptor.

Here are some ideas on superlatives that can work well in your headlines.

Positive:

- **Best**
- **Always**
- **Most**

- **Greatest**
- **Strongest**

Negative:

- **Never**
- **Nothing**
- **Worst**
- **Stop**
- **Avoid**

8. Speak to one person.

When you are writing, use the word "you" instead of "me" or "we." Using "you" in your headline is personal and grabs your audience's attention!

9. Promise a solution to a problem.

Here are a few examples you can use:

- How to_____ That Will Help You Increase_____
- Why____Will Make You a Better_____
- 10 Rules for Maximizing_____ For_____
- 7 Ways To Get More from _____ and _____
- Avoid These 10 Mistakes When You_____

Now that you know what you want to write about, and have a few tips on how to write it, just how long should your content be?

The ideal length for every type of content

If a little content is good then a lot of content is better … right? Not necessarily. The fact is, your readers have a limited, attention span, and you want to hit their sweet spot, not saturate them and run the risk of pushing them away.

But how to do that? MarketingProfs offers a few suggestions on the matter. They touch on social-media outlets from Twitter to Google and provide specific, content-lengths for everything from a headline to a blog post, and more. Check out their recommendations below: (http://www.marketingprofs.com/chirp/2016/29671/the-ideal-word-counts-for-social-media-posts-infographic)

Twitter:

100 characters is the perfect length for a single tweet on Twitter and receive 17% more engagement.

Keep it short, sweet and to-the-point.

Facebook:

The ideal Facebook post is 40 characters or fewer and receive 86% more engagement than longer posts. The second most ideal post is 80 characters or fewer which receives 66% more engagement than longer posts.

Google+:

The highest performing posts on Google+ are headlines that are 60 characters or fewer. The ideal length of a Google+ body content is 200-440 words.

Pinterest

When it comes to Pinterest, 200-character descriptions on Pinterest receive the most repins and pins that feature a call to action earn 80% more engagements.

Blog posts:

How much is too much? As a general rule, blogs longer typically rank higher in Google, but MarketingProfs (source link above) tells us that readers are generally willing to remain with an article for 1,600 words. That's approximately a seven-minute read. Blog posts that are longer than 1,500 words receive an average of 68% more tweets than shorter posts and 23% more Facebook likes.

Are you surprised by these results?

While this information may come as a shock, it will help you write more interesting headlines that get read… along with the rest of your content.

Now, onto your social-media strategy…

Chapter 6

* * *

Honing Your Social Media Strategy

A few years ago, my parents called me up and said, "Katie, we found this box in our garage." Now, I haven't lived at home in some time, so I was a little curious what was in this box. They brought it over to my house, and when I opened it, there was a lot of stuff in there… kind of a walk down memory-lane which included my Girl Scout badge, high school photos, and other, fun stuff. And as I got to the bottom of the box, there was another box!

It was full of letters and took me back to when I was 15 years-old. At that time, my best friend, Lori, moved from California to Denver. And when you're 15 years-old, and your best friend moves 2000 miles away, it's pretty traumatic. Now, this was before email and Facebook so we kept in touch by writing letters to each other, and it was really fun.

Well, the memories flooded back as I went through the letters, and I even found some pictures of clothes, too. And I had to giggle because I remembered going to the mall as a teenager with Lori. We would buy clothes, bring them home and lay them out on the bed. Then, we would take pictures, develop the film, put them in an envelope, and share them with each other. It was a type of social networking before social-networking online was born!

I tell this story because while it is so wonderful to have all of those physical items from the past, it also shows how far we have come with technology. Today, we are living in an amazing time where social has really transformed how we communicate, keep in touch and build our businesses. Not only can we talk to people via phone, a handwritten note (which still works, by the way), and email, but now, we have this other tool that really, enhances how we keep in touch with others and build relationships and our businesses. After all, we can contact anyone in the world at any time with an Internet connection, and most of us are walking around with an iPhone or Android mobile device. That type of technology didn't even exist just a few years ago. And now, we wouldn't imagine leaving our house without it!

Plus, social media has changed the way news spreads. You can read about something online faster than it appears on the radio, television news or in print. And I'm sure a lot of us have experienced this through events that have happened in your life. For example, think of the year when the Boston-Marathon tragedy occurred. Within moments of the bombs going off and everything happening, the American Red Cross had Google pages, Person Finder (I'm looking for someone. I have information on someone), and other tools set up to help people.

Social media is a communications channel

I think one of the first things to understand when it comes to thinking about and honing a social-media strategy is to understand that it's not just a marketing channel. Social is really a communications channel. Sometimes, social gets lumped into this big, marketing bucket with print advertising, direct-mail, in-person visits, and whatever else the marketing department is responsible for working on at the present time.

But it's essential to realize how important social-media really is, especially when you're trying to target Gen X, Gen Y, the Millennials, and, quite frankly, any age. There's an enormous amount of time that's spent on social media. Every 15 minutes there are over 49 million posts. To be precise 49,433,000 or 3 million posts per minute.There are 500,000 Facebook "likes" every minute!

(http://www.jeffbullas.com/2015/04/17/21-awesome-facebook-facts-and-statistics-you-need-to-check-out)

It's pretty incredible and makes you wonder what we are doing with our time!

Well, this is where being intentional comes into play, especially in the real-estate industry. If you are just starting with social-media, or have been using it for some time, ask yourself what you really need to focus on, what you want to achieve and who you want to connect with. This makes a real difference so here are a few things to think about…

Infuse your personality - be true to who you are

What are you passionate about? What are you comfortable sharing? Is it wine? Is it food? Is it dogs? Is it cats? Is it your kids?

You might think, "What's the big deal?" But, that's how people connect. They want to know more about you than just what's going on with your business. Sure, people may work with you because of your experience and your expertise, but they connect with you because of who you are. Share some personal insights and be authentic. Show the flaws, the good days and the bad days. People will appreciate this.

Watch your grammar

Sometimes, we think that social is just about posting things quickly. But don't forget to check your grammar before you click "post." Grammar counts. It tells people a lot about you and your business.

Be compelling

What kinds of topics will get you to comment, like or share? This is an important thing. Remember, on Facebook, you're competing with everyone's friends, and their family and everything they're posting. Post something that is compelling to your audience.

Consistency counts

This is big. So many times, I see what's called a Facebook graveyard, which is a Facebook page that hasn't been tended to in some time. And frequently, this is because there's no action or consistent posts to that page. If you start using social media, post on a consistent basis.

How to launch a successful, social-media strategy

With all this in mind, you've decided to formulate and launch your new, social-media campaign. Now, exactly how do you do that?

To start, you need to do your due diligence in order to figure out your resources and goals before you can roll out a successful, social-media strategy.

Remember that a complete, social-media strategy is not simply a vow to become more active on Facebook and Twitter. This is a complete package with the end-goal of building your brand and business.

Here are a few questions to help you start off in the right direction:

- What are your goals?
- How do they tie into your company goals?
- What are the best social-networks to meet these goals?
- Who is your target audience?
- Who is your ideal customer?
- How do you plan to draw and retain customers?
- How will ROI be measured?
- Will you outsource your social media or keep it in-house?

Now comes research. Check out a variety of social-media sites to determine which ones are right for you. When you're looking at these sites, check out your competitors while identifying your target audience. You're then ready to start building relationships as you follow the online conversation. Which blogs and individuals are relevant to your business? Figure this out, and make sure you know what they're saying.

At this point, you'll want to jump in and join the conversation. This includes fielding questions on LinkedIn, joining Twitter chats and offering insight on forums and blogs. At the same time, you can bolster these relationships by including in-person interaction in your strategy. Meet with people offline, attend conferences, and make other, personal gestures to give yourself a face behind the online presence.

Once you're a part of the online community, it's time to figure out how your efforts are paying off. Are your Facebook fans growing in number? Are you seeing comments increase? When it comes to conversations about your brand, is the chatter more positive or negative? How many contacts have you made? How much traffic is your website seeing?

All of these questions offer critical feedback as to whether your social-media strategy is working, and in turn, you can use this information to fine-tune your campaign.

Here's where you engage in trial-and-error to find out what works best. As you continue to experiment, you'll find out what's worth your effort and what's not. Keep in mind that social media is not one-size-fits all. You need to tweak your personal campaign in order to not only best suit y your business, but also yourself as the owner and operator.

And once you're up and running, how do you save time and effort moving forward. Well, here are some tips to streamline the process...

Make the connection: streamlining your social media

Here's the beauty of social media... You're not limited to any number of profiles on different networks.

Here's the difficulty of social media... Same thing!

We've got a world full of choices when it comes to our social-media platforms, but how do you organize it all?

It's important to remember that, while you can easily share the same content across several, different networks, the differences between those networks make it crucial that you tweak your content in order to be appropriate for different audiences. For example, while you can certainly post the same article on Facebook that you post on Twitter, Facebook is more conversational than Twitter, which is shorter and might merit a hashtag.

Here's the thing. You don't need to reinvent the wheel each time in order to make your content appropriate for each social-network. A few slight changes can make all the difference. Let's stick with the example of Facebook versus Twitter. Say you want to post a news article. You have room on Facebook to offer commentary and solicit feedback, but on Twitter you only have 140 characters. This is where you have to figure out the heart of what you want to share, and adjust your Facebook commentary to fit Twitter.

Essentially, it's great to streamline your social-media activity, but in doing so, you don't want to lose the nuances that differentiate each network and differentiate your audience as well.

Now let's look at some of the applications that can help you bring all your social-networking profiles together to work smarter for you:

Bit.ly

This is best known for shortening links so that you can post them on Twitter, but Bit.ly offers more than that. Its other resources include real-time analytics, click-tracking and bookmarking your favorite sites. Bit.ly works across multiple platforms and it's free.

Buffer

Here's a one-click program that allows you to share content and schedule posts over many of the major social-networks, including Facebook, Google+, LinkedIn, and Twitter. This option allows you to have consistent posting throughout the day since you can schedule posts ahead of time. It's free, but just for a short period, and then there is a paid version.

HootSuite and Sprout Social

These are two of the most well-known applications of their type. These platforms provide access via a web-based dashboard to multiple, social-media networks, where you can also track conversations and measure campaign results. You can also schedule posts on all platforms and measure analytics. Both of these platforms have a free and a paid version.

Great! You are well on your way to successful, social-media activities. Here are more insights...

Chapter 7

•   •   •

Social Media Time Management: How to Curate, Create and Promote Content

Time is everything and time is our most precious resource. So, how can we be most effective with our time when it comes to social media, stay up to date with the latest and greatest, build engagement with our customers and clients, generate new leads - AND do everything else we need to do in our day-to-day job?

Systems are key. You have to have some type of system or your best laid plans - will always go astray! For a lot of you (myself included) - you need to put things on your calendar, otherwise they will not happen. But, before you can do that, you really need to be clear on your brand and ask yourself:

•   Which channels will you will focus on?
•   How will your channels work together?
•   What is the audience for those channels?

But, are you asking the right question? So often, the question people ask me is, "Should I be on Facebook or should I be on (insert social network here.)" But, that's not the right question. The right question should be, "What social networks should I focus on that will build my community and build my business?" Also, what platforms do you enjoy the most?

When you can answer those questions, you can then put on your calendar when you are going to do three major things:

1. Curate content
2. Create content
3. Promote content

So let's break this down a little further...

Curating content. Whether you are building your Facebook presence, creating unique Stories for Snapchat, or building a community on Instagram - curating is probably going to be a part of your process. As much as I love original content, I found that most brands are going to need to have a system in place for curating and finding really great content (links, videos or graphics from other sources) that they can then share with their social networks.

For me, I spend a few minutes every morning looking for great content to curate. I have been doing this for years now - so it's just a part of my morning coffee routine and usually takes no more than 10-15 minutes - 4 or 5 days a week, but it looks a little something like this:

First, it's important to note what audiences I am curating content for.

Typically, when I am curating, I am scanning for content that I could share to:

- My personal Facebook profile. 80% of what I post here is personal - but if I run across something super timely for social media (or funny) - I love to share it here.
- My Facebook business page. For this page, I primarily post content from my blog, but to fill-in on days where I don't have content I look for

curated content to schedule such as: funny memes, inspirational quotes, or highly shareable links. Using my Facebook Insights - I can see which types of posts get the most engagement and I post more of those.

- My 3 Facebook groups. I have my private coaching group - where I tend to post breaking news first; my social media manager group - where I post articles about social media management; and my #GetSocialSmart group - where I post a variety of articles on social media marketing in general

- Twitter. I like to post and schedule timely articles on social media, digital marketing, tech, mobile, marketing, real estate and branding. I use HootSuite for a lot of this type of scheduling for Twitter.

- Instagram. For this channel, I am looking for other great Instagram content to repost or re-share. I like using RepostApp to do this.

- Pinterest. I like to pin 3-5 new pins a day relevant to my brand; social media marketing.

- Periscope and Facebook Live. I love to use these platforms to talk about breaking news on the social channels, so as I'm curating - I am looking for that breaking news to share that day on live video.

- Snapchat. Snapchat fills in a lot of the gaps for me and it's been fun to share a quick tip here or there. I haven't curated a ton of of content yet for Snapchat - but for right now, it's been fun to watch how people are using the platform.

So now that I know WHO I am curating for - it's a lot easier to do this quickly each day. By the way, as mentioned above, I like to do this generally 4-5 times a week every morning. By doing this - I stay top of mind with my industry and I can make sure the content I am curating is fresh and relevant.

Here's my quick 4-step system each morning for curating content:

1. **Email newsletters.** I scan my email and click on a few industry email newsletters and share and/or schedule content to the above platforms if there is something interesting and of value. I love subscribing to

SmartBrief newsletters - you can subscribe to various industries and they always email great content.

2. **Twitter lists.** I love using Twitter lists. I have created a ton of Twitter lists (which can be public or private) which are great sources for curating content. I recommend creating Twitter lists based on interests and topics relevant to your brand. For example, I have a social media list, a real estate news list, a client list, and many more. I pick 2 or 3 lists each morning and quickly scan and either re-tweet immediately or I use content I find on the other channels listed above.

3. **BuzzSumo.** It's a great way to find the very latest content that is relevant to your brand. Looking for something that gets a high level of Facebook shares? Looking to see the latest trending article on a certain topic in the last 24 hours or week or month? Looking to set up alerts for content? BuzzSumo is extremely robust - I only spend a few minutes here a day looking for the best content to share.

4. **Instagram.** I scan my Instagram feed every morning and like and/or comment on many posts - typically 5-10 or so. I have found that by posting to my Instagram account 2-3 times a day along with engaging with my followers - it has had a profound effect on my following. In fact, I have more than doubled my Instagram community in just the last few months by ramping up how often I post. As mentioned above, I like to use RepostApp to repost and reshare content that is relevant to my brand.

In addition, I have three small things that make a huge difference when scheduling some of this curated content:

- I never schedule it for more than a day or two out - the point here is to be fresh and relevant.
- I always credit the source AND the reporter. On Twitter I make sure to tag the source and the reporter (sometimes you need to Google the reporter's Twitter handle) - but I found this extra step is huge in engagement with the reporter!

- I share links to multiple networks. Very rarely does a curated link get shared to all my social platforms - but many times, it may get shared in a Facebook Group, then scheduled to Tweet out later that day and also pinned to one of my Pinterest boards. Or, maybe I'll share a link on my Facebook Business Page and then that becomes inspiration for a Snapchat story or Live Video. I am all about not reinventing the wheel!

Ok, so now you've curated some killer content but here is where the real heavy lifting comes into play: creating content!

Just like curating, you need a system for creating content - but before you can have a system, you need to think about what type of content you are going to create.

Created content could be:

- Blog posts - on your own site or another site like Medium or LinkedIn
- Video - DIY short videos or longer-form professionally edited videos
- Live Video – Periscope, Facebook Live or Instagram Live
- Graphics - Ideal for Instagram and other social networks, but will also be needed to promote other content (i.e. blogs, videos, live video, etc.)

You may decide to create all or some of what is listed above.

I have always been of the school of thought that the best type of content is content that lives on your site. For us, we have consistently created blog posts and published at least one per week since our site launched in 2013. If you click through many of our blog posts - you'll see most are written but many have a video component within the post or a link to a Live Video that I did on that same topic.

I have found by repurposing content on multiple platforms, it extends the life of your content and reaches more people.

Keep it simple!

Create a blog calendar (using a Spreadsheet and/or a Calendar) and lay out your topics for the next 3 months. These may change - but put them down so you have a road map. Then, you need to decide what day you are going to publish that piece of content. I recommend being consistent whether is is a blog post every Wednesday, or a Blab show every Tuesday - whatever it is - people will tune in and watch and share when you get on a regular schedule.

Once you've laid out your road map, you need to put in your calendar when you will create this content. This includes the actual content and then the supporting materials - for example, for each blog post, I want to include screenshots, additional images or graphics and a featured images. For me, I like to create content either early morning or late at night. You need to find chunks of uninterrupted time to create and write - or a time that works best for live video.

If you are just starting down the road of social media for your business, you may only have time to create one blog post a month or maybe one or two short videos. That's ok. We all start somewhere, and being consistent is better than suffering from analysis paralysis.

For us, we create a blog post once a week which is our pillar piece of content, but I also create 5-7 live video shows a week and other shorter form video content either specifically for my Facebook Groups or Instagram or Snapchat. It's important to note that we have a small team here at KLC, but a lot of what I talking about in this post is something I love to do - it keeps me fresh and it brings me a tremendous amount of joy.

Now that you have curated and created content - it's all about promoting it!

We talked a bit about scheduling when we talked about curating content. For curated content I either post in the moment or schedule a day or two in advance each day. For created content though, our process is a bit more extensive.

Depending on the content - we go through a process to promote that content. Someone asked me the other day, "do people really read blogs?" And I smiled and said, "yes, but you have to tell them about it and promote your posts - otherwise most people never see it." And if you think about your own behavior, there are probably few sites you just go to on a regular basis to read their content - for most of you, you see it in your Newsfeed as you are scrolling by.

Our 11-step process for promoting our pillar, weekly content includes:

1. Sending a dedicated email about the post to our email list
2. Sharing the post on our Facebook page and boosting the post or running a Facebook ad promoting that post.
3. Sharing the post on some or all of our Facebook groups (as appropriate)
4. Sharing the post to Twitter and pinning the Tweet.
5. Add this link to our Edgar library for Twitter. (I love MeetEdgar for created content - it allows us to 'drip' content out over the course of time as we see fit.)
6. Share the link to LinkedIn (sometimes we repost the blog post in it's entirety to LinkedIn as a published post.)
7. Pin the link to any relevant Pinterest boards.
8. Share the link on Instagram by creating a graphic and changing out the dedicated link you are allowed to the blog post of the week.
9. Including the link in our weekly email newsletter

10. Privately sharing on social media to 5-10 friends or colleagues whom I think would enjoy it (using Facebook Messenger.)
11. Rinse and repeat as needed.

Remember, you are your own best promoter - so get the word out about your content! At the end of the day - great content is going to bring you a GREAT community and GREAT clients or customers. I can't tell you how many people who come to my website to request more information to work with me - already feel like they "know" me because of the great content we have consistently been producing for years.

So, let's put it all together - how much TIME should this all take? It really depends! For us, it breaks down like this weekly:

- 1-hour or so curating
- 1-2 hours or so scheduling and promoting
- 3-5 hours (or more!) creating blog, live video, graphics and recorded video content

Is that a lot? Less than you thought? There really is no magic formula. For some of you - this entire process could take an hour or two - and for others it's an entire full-time job.

As mentioned above, the time you spend on this could be more or less depending on where you are at with your business. But keep this in mind - it doesn't have to take a lot of time. But, (and here is the big BUT....) it does take focused time and specific goals to make this effective.

We can not forget about engagement! Of course - the giant part in this entire conversation is engagement and building your community.

You can't curate, create or promote great content and then walk away! For me, engagement happens throughout the day - the important thing for me is #NoTweetLeftBehind - so once I've put this great content out there, it's important to me to respond to anyone and everyone who shares it, tweets it, mentions me, tags me - on all social platforms. It's also important to be in the moment and share what others around you are sharing.

Social media is never, ever a one-way, promotion-only place to be. When done right, social media is a two-way street.

In fact, one of the best strategies for social media is to think about how you can recognize others publicly...

Chapter 8

●　●　●

The Power of Recognizing People Publicly

It's no secret that the savviest of business people have turned to social-media platforms in order to market themselves and build their brand. However, while many try to take advantage of these hot trends and use them to broadcast their message, not all fully reap the rewards.

What is the "secret sauce" when it comes to effectively marketing your brand on social media?

There is a power of thanking people publicly in this day and age of social media. Sure, there are still opportunities and moments for one-to-one conversation like a handwritten note, phone call or private email, but in this day-and-age, there is also the opportunity to make public what might once would have been a private accolade. Can you be a good-finder and look for moments of opportunity to publicly recognize someone?

On the flip side, more and more people turn to Twitter or Facebook when they have a negative experience. Where again, in the past, perhaps they would have written a letter to the CEO or made a phone call.

What's the power and reasoning behind "going public?"

One of the biggest reasons is to give that person recognition in a public forum, in front of all of their friends and colleagues.

As an example, if you are a sales professional, at some point you participated in sales meetings where the manager discussed goals and recognized a few individuals with a round of applause. Well, those sales meetings happen, but now they can also "happen" online via social. Imagine the power of recognizing your top sales-person publicly on Facebook or Twitter – tagging them in a post and then making a very genuine remark. Now, that person feels amazing, and you have recognized them among their peers and friends.

I also think we have a lot of moments in our day-to-day life. These may seem like mundane moments, but I look at these moments as opportunities to tell the story of who I am, and when it makes sense, to recognize someone else.

I experienced the power of this recently…

Experience #1

After a long travel week, I tweeted Air Canada a "thank you" tweet about the good service I experienced at the Victoria Airport. I didn't have to do that, but I wanted all of my followers on Twitter to know about my great experience and to publicly give accolades.

To my delight, within moments, Air Canada replied with a kind tweet, which really impressed me even more, because they were listening. "@katielance Music to our ears Katie! Thank you for sharing the #kudos with us. We'll pass along your comments to the right team for you /lb— Air Canada (@AirCanada)"

And here's an important note – I never expect anything in return when I post something publicly to recognize someone or something.

But, I will say, it is the cherry-on-top when they notice and respond. As I always like to say, "just because you aren't there, doesn't mean the conversation isn't happening!" And this is truer than ever before because of social media.

I found that when you do something nice for someone, or recognize someone for something, it is like a snowball, and it comes back to you tenfold.

Experience #2

If you read my story earlier about United Airlines, you will particularly like this story. Recently, I was on a United flight to Orlando. I had expected Wi-Fi on the plane, but after taking my seat, I was told that the Internet connection would be unavailable on this six-hour flight from San Francisco. A bit annoyed, since I was planning on working on this flight, I tweeted United Airlines right before take-off.

When we landed in Orlando, the flight attendant got on the speaker and said, "Katie Lance, please see a United representative as soon as you can once you de-plane." I had no idea what to expect. Upon leaving the plane, I was greeted by a gentleman with a gift bag in his hand. He said to me, "Katie Lance, on behalf of the United Marketing Team we have a gift for you!"

I couldn't believe it! I was speechless. Inside the gift bag were some really thoughtful travel-gifts purchased from Brookstone. But even more amazing, there was a hand-written card from the marketing person apologizing for the lack of Wi-Fi and expressing her appreciation for my business.

I couldn't believe it! I was so impressed with the thoughtfulness that I immediately tweeted United airlines. And then later that evening, I did a live broadcast on Periscope sharing this amazing act of care with the world and taking things a step further.

There are so many benefits to taking your customer service to the next level by using social media. When you surprise and delight people – the benefits are exponential!

The big key here is authenticity and intentions.

You have to have the best of intentions when you publicly thank someone. It can't be because you want to look good on your social networks or gain a lot of "atta boys" or "atta girls." It has to come from the heart, and be genuine. It has to be something you'd say the exact same way if no one was listening.

Have you had opportunity to thank someone or recognize someone publicly?

How did it go? How was their reaction?

I encourage you to be more aware as you move forward with social-media and your posts. Look for moments to be a good finder and to reach out and connect with people in a meaningful way.

Now, how to use blogs in social media...

Chapter 9

●　●　●

How to Get More Traction with Your Blog

Having your own voice, your own stamp on the world, is one of the most important things any business owner can do to differentiate himself or herself. With this in mind, do you ever feel like you are spinning your wheels with Facebook? If so, one of the number one questions you can ask is, "what type of content are you creating?"

Whether it is a written or video blog, creating content is one of the best things a business can do to tell the story of their brand, showcase the culture of the company and connect with their audience. However, blogs don't come with built-in audiences. Once you start creating content, you may wonder, "Is anyone reading this?" And if often feels this way for most people starting off in blogging.

So how do you get people to read and share your content?

Here are a few things that make a huge difference in getting more traction with your blog.

Life is content

If you're just starting in blogging, try to look at your life as content. For example, if I'm out speaking somewhere, I'll snap a photo and put it on Facebook.

I'll also share things about coffee or wine, or things that I see when I'm out and about and find beautiful or interesting. The key here is to instill a mindset where you are looking for those moments of inspiration. Whether it's something beautiful, or touching, or moving, or funny... that's really powerful stuff.

Plan ahead, but be flexible

I've tried probably every single content strategy known to man and found that typically what works best for me and my team is two things: a Google Doc and Google Calendar. This helps us have an idea of the type of content we're going to put out for the next three to six months. It's structured, but is also flexible and allows us to make as many changes as necessary.

Ask yourself: who are you trying to attract?

What type of customer or client are you trying to attract? Many times, we make the mistake of thinking we can be all things to all people.

I believe that narrowing down your ideal client and then creating content specifically for them is huge for content-strategy success. The type of content you create is the type of client you are going to attract. Again, it's important to be intentional with your efforts.

Write for one person.

When you create content, try not to sound like you are shouting to the masses. What I've found is that if you can focus on your ideal client and write for that one person, it's going to make your content much more personable and compelling.

Edit ruthlessly

This is important. When I blog I will write, write, write, and then go back and edit ruthlessly. I look at grammar, style, tone, length, and more. And just how long should your blog be? There are different schools of thought when it comes to blog post-length. I personally think people have a short attention span so I try to keep my posts short and sweet, usually, between 500-600 words.

Don't forget the basics

Whatever industry you're in, remember that there are always people looking for the basic information. As much as I love the advanced stuff, I also understand that a lot of my audience is looking for more basic tips.

Consider the medium

Which source is the best for your content? This is something I take into consideration when I'm blogging, creating recorded videos or creating live videos on Periscope, Facebook Live or any other platform. Think about what type of content makes the most sense for you and your brand. Now, you and your brand are going to be many things, but think about what aspects might be better suited for different platforms.

How do you get your blog readers coming back time and time again?

Get aggressive with Twitter

Twitter moves fast. What you post today is often forgotten (or not seen) tomorrow. Tweet each of your blog posts multiple times. Use a tool like HootSuite to schedule them over the course of a few days, or weeks, depending on the topic.

And ensure people aren't leaving your site unnecessarily. Set all links to "open in a new window" so that visitors won't have to leave your site to view them.

Also, use tools like Click-to-Tweet to embed tweetable sentences throughout your post – prompting readers to tweet them out!

The Amazon "trick"

Another way to keep readers on your site is to end each post with something to the effect of "See additional posts like this," and then include two-to three-links of other, relevant blog-posts on your site.

Ask for the share

If you have highlighted people or businesses within your blog post, make sure to email the link to them, and ask them to share it with their network. This is especially key if you are interviewing someone on your blog!

Divide and conquer

If it's appropriate, you may consider breaking up one, large chunk of information into several posts, grouping relevant information together in each.

Advertise

Posts that are specific to a particular audience-group are ideal to run as ads on Facebook. These are not boosted posts, but rather, Facebook ads that run in the newsfeed on desktop and mobile sites as well as on the right-hand side of Facebook and on Facebook's partner, mobile-sites.

Call-to-action

Finally, seasonal posts are timely and can really boost your audience. You might consider adding a call-to-action at the end of the blog post. Try, "Post a picture of your Thanksgiving meal on my Facebook page for the chance to win a Starbucks card," or something to that effect.

While creating a vibrant, blog community requires a little investment of time and creativity, it'll be worth it when you see the pay-off!

9 quick and easy blog ideas

Looking to beef up your blog but need some fresh ideas to add to your content calendar?

Here are five of my favorite types of posts that can help jump-start your creative juices:

1. Q/A

Who can you contact to do a quick interview or ask 5-10 questions? How about someone in your industry or someone local? Especially if you are just building your online presence, interviewing someone, and then tagging them in social-media updates when you promote it, can be a great strategy to provide good content. And most likely, that person will share it on their social-networks too!

What questions do you get asked repeatedly? Write about those! When you're brainstorming for your blogging calendar, think about the frequently-asked questions you receive in your business. Regardless of the business you're in, whether it's a big company or you work for yourself, you're sure to have some questions that you are asked often. Leverage those questions by creating content to answer them.

2. Checklist

Everyone loves a checklist. What types of checklists can you create for your industry? How about a moving-day checklist if you are a Realtor? Or a packing-checklist is you are in the travel industry? Or a checklist for the don't-miss wineries in Napa if you are in the wine industry?

Checklists are simple to create and easy content to digest and share!

3. A Collection.

Why not do a weekly or monthly round-up of some of your favorite articles you've read? Make sure to include links back to the author and publication. And when you are promoting this blog post on social media, don't forget to tag them too! This is a great way to build relationships with the local media, be perceived as an expert and bring great content to your readers. Looking for inspiration? Social Media Examiner does a great weekly round-up!

4. How-To

Are you an expert on something? Why not write "how-to" articles as part of your blog content? For me, I get asked about the ins-and-outs of social media, so crafting "how-to's" for specific things within social media makes sense for me.

One of my most-read blog posts is a how-to LinkedIn article about organizing LinkedIn contacts. Also, I love using Jing to capture screenshots, which are hugely important for how-to articles.

5. Infographics

Are you in an industry that is heavily data-driven? Perhaps, you are in the financial or mortgage industry? For many people, data is very dry so how can you spice it up for social media? *Sites like infogr.am or visual.ly offer great tools to create infographics!*

6. Lessons learned

What are lessons you've learned in your business? By sharing these lessons, it's going to do two things. One, it's going to connect you with your audience through shared experiences and/or relatable circumstances. Secondly, it will help you tell your story by showcasing where you've been and how far you've grown.

7. The basics of what you do

Don't underestimate the power of blogging about the basics of what you do. This applies to every industry, regardless of what it is. Think about the things you learned when you first entered your industry. It's great to offer advanced tips and tricks to your audience, but don't forget about the basics.

8. Snackable content

What is snackable content? Think quick tips and tricks – small things that people can easily read and digest. When you think about how people are consuming content these days, short and sweet is often best.

9. Behind-the-scenes

Give people a sneak-peek of what it is that you do. People love seeing behind-the-scenes of your business!

You have great content. Where do you post it?

Once you create this content, where should it live? I'm a firm believer that your website is the best place to post your content. Google loves when you're consistently updating your content. When your website is fresh, it really helps to increase your Google rankings. My recommendation is to host your blog on a WordPress site.

Don't have a blog on your website? Another great option is LinkedIn. It's very simple to create a blog post on LinkedIn. And the great part about doing so is that once you've published, a notification will be sent to everyone you're connected to on LinkedIn. LinkedIn blog-posts also have their own unique URL, which you can then share on other networks such as Facebook, Twitter and others.

Another great option is Medium. Medium is a fantastic platform for easily creating blog content, quickly and efficiently.

You have your content, what about visuals?

Chapter 10

• • •

How to Create Your Ultimate Blogging Calendar

Let me know if this sounds familiar. You know you should probably blog or create content and you agree that it sounds like a good idea, but this is where you get stuck...

You get stuck in making it happen week after week.

You get stuck on what to blog about, where to blog, what format it should be in and you wonder, "does anyone really read blogs anymore?"

Blogging isn't a new conversation, but it's important to talk about the why behind blogging and why you need to think about it even more.

There is more information being thrown at us in every which way than ever before. But, there is a real need for relevant and timely content – more than ever.

I've been blogging since 2009 in one form or another and I can tell you that the results have made a huge impact on my business and in my bottom line.

The value though is not just blogging when you feel like it, or when the mood strikes - it's doing so on a consistent basis.

And for a lot of marketers and business owners, this is the challenging part. I can tell you from personal experience; I have blogged with a calendar and without a calendar - and the times I have used a calendar is when my business has exploded.

Here is why:

- **Creating a blog calendar makes blogging a priority and a habit.** When something becomes a habit, it's just something you do as part of your routine - like brushing your teeth. The key to getting business and leads from a blog - is that people come to expect it week after week, month after month, and year after year. You are building trust when you are consistently providing great content.
- **Creating a blog calendar gets you out of the 'here and now' and forces you to think ahead.** Too often, people who blog create blog content when they become inspired or when there is something to write about. What happens? Your blog becomes inconsistent in how often you are publishing which hurts your readership (and ultimately your business) and it hurts the balance of content on your blog. By thinking 30-90 days ahead, you can have a good balance of the type of content that is relevant to your business.
- **Creating a blog calendar forces you to be consistent in effort - which means your readers (your clients, prospects and customers) will be consistent in their response to your blog.** For example, we publish our email newsletter every Saturday and have for years - I can't tell you how many people comment to me about how they like receiving it Saturday morning. We are creatures of habit and when you consistently blog, people will come to expect it and LOOK for it!

Consistent effort = consistent reward!

How do you go about creating a blog calendar if you have never created one before?

There are two simple options that I think work the best:

Option 1: Spreadsheet. You can create a spreadsheet using Google Documents or Excel. This format is great because you can see at a glance all of your topics and dates in one easy to read location. Our blog calendar is in a Google Document spreadsheet so everyone on our team can see it at any time.

I'd recommend if you go this route - simple is better. I prefer just two columns: topic and due date. If you have more people on your team you may want to add additional columns like: first draft due, graphics due, etc. But, if you are a one-person show and just starting - keep it simple! Even with our team - I went back to a very simple spreadsheet with topic and due date. We publish once a week - every Wednesday, so I know the day or two before I will be working on it to get everything written, proofed, etc.

Option 2: Calendar. Some people prefer to use an actual written calendar, or others like to use an Outlook or Google Calendar. We used a Google Calendar for awhile, but I felt for my needs - I preferred looking at my entire blog calendar in a spreadsheet. I do, however, like to use my calendar to block off time to write, and I also use it for any other content creation I do that may end up on the blog like recorded or live video content.

Ultimately, you have to do what works best for you and the key, just like anything, is implementation. It has to be something that is easy to use and easy to access.

Other successful bloggers swear by CoSchedule, an editorial calendar plugin for WordPress or a tool like Trello for visual collaboration. Again, you have to use what works best for you. For me, simple is better!

It's also important to understand that your blog is a moving target. So, although you want to think 30-60-90 days out with your blog calendar, it's ok to shift and re-arrange topics as needed.

Now, once you've created a simple spreadsheet or calendar, how do you decide which content to put on there? How do you know what people will want to read?

When I am working on my own blog calendar or I am consulting for a client, there are a few steps I take:

- What is your brand all about? I always start by brainstorming words that showcase my specialty or expertise - and these become the basis for my topics. For example, my brainstorm word list includes:
  - Social media and social media strategy
  - Social media time management
  - Facebook tips
  - Facebook advertising
  - Instagram and Pinterest
  - Snapchat, Periscope and Facebook Live
  - Content marketing, content strategy, blogging

This list are all topics I am completely comfortable writing about because this is my expertise - and this is what clients hire me to consult with them about! Notice this list does not include things like: graphic design or public relations. Even though I have experience in those - that is not my brand and those are not the type of clients I am trying to attract.

So, what type of clients or customers are you trying to attract? What content could you provide that would help your clients and customers? Remember, blog content isn't just the same content people can read any-where – the difference in a blog post is that it includes your opinion and your voice.

For example, if you are a real estate agent – you may write a blog about the three ways you can get your home ready for the market, OR you can write that same blog post with those three tips and include a personal story of a client and what you specifically recommend and why. If you can back that up with examples – then you have the formula for a great blog post.

Here are a few no-fail tips I use to jump-start my blog calendar

- Sit with a blank pen and paper and brainstorm 20-40 topics. There is no right or wrong, just start writing topics that are of interest to you and may be of interest to your readers. Stuck? Look in your Sent email and see what questions you are answering all the time!
- Ask yourself, "What keeps yours clients or customers up at night?" What is their pain point? These answers are great topics for you!
- Plan around key dates, holidays and the seasonality of your industry. I always think about things like the holidays, back to school, tax-time, etc. Context is king.

Here's the great news - blog posts don't have to be the same every time you publish them. Here are a few of my favorite types of posts:

- **Lists.** People love a good list! Think in terms of 3, 5 or 7 tips - this makes it easy to write and easy for people to read and share.
- **How-to's.** What do you know how to do that others don't? How about: "How to list your house for sale with an agent?" or "How to hire the right real estate agent?" These may seem like basic questions, but for a lot of people - these are exactly the types of questions that keep them up at night!
- **Checklists.** What checklist could you create that would be of value to your clients? How about: "Your 30-Day Moving Checklist" or "Getting Your Kids Ready for the Big Move: Your Checklist!"

- **Q/A or an interview:** Reach out to local business owners or others in your industry. Let them know you want to feature them on your blog. If you are a new blogger, this is a great way to make connections and leverage their social footprint. Make it easy for the other person to respond - send them 5-7 questions, format your blog post and once you publish - send them the link and ask them to share it out to their networks!
- **Company news.** New product updates, new team members, any announcements - put it on your blog!
- **Weekly round-ups.** We all are consuming so much content. How about a post once a week with your top 5 articles of the week. Social Media Examiner does a fantastic round-up every week and you could too based on your industry!
- **Product reviews.** Have a new iPhone you love? How about a new Drone or a new App? Do a quick product review. Talk about the product, why you love it, what you use it for, and how people can purchase it!

Lastly, the question I get asked all the time about blogging is where to host a blog. I think your own website is always best, and I always recommend WordPress. But, if you don't have that capability and you are ready to start today, I recommend starting with Medium or LinkedIn.

Ok, so now that you have started brainstorming content and have started to draft your calendar - now the real work begins!

Remember, consistent effort equals consistent reward. Also remember, that a blog is not just words on a page - it's your opinion, it's YOU. I know there are hundreds if not thousands of social media books you could be reading right now - but you are choosing to read my book because you want to know my thoughts and my ideas. I never take that for granted, which is why it's so important for me to not just regurgitate what you could read anywhere but to give my expertise that my readers and my clients are looking for.

I can also tell you from personal experience, that the leads that come to me through my website are generally so much BETTER because many times they've been reading my blog and consuming my content for years.

Instead of having to 'sell myself' every time I get on the phone with a prospect - many times they know exactly who I am from reading my blog, and they are selling themselves on why I should work with them. Imagine that!

Chapter 11

●　●　●

The Power of Visual Marketing with Instagram and Pinterest

Visuals are one of the most important pieces when putting together a content strategy for your social-media. But many people are overwhelmed by the thought of adding photos, videos and other graphics to their posts. Well, in this chapter, I want to teach you how to use images in your social media as easily as possible.

To start, let's talk about stock photos. And before you skip to the next chapter, note that a lot has changed with stock photos. Yes, there are still some not-so-great stock photos out there. But, finding great stock-photos that are relevant to your brand and that you can use for your website, blog and social-media channels are priceless!

Where do you find graphics to use? Well, instead of just using Google images (which may or not be copyright-protected), check out these awesome, jaw-dropping and beautiful stock-photo-sites.

Look for images you want to use, and then read each site to check on their rules for using these photos for commercial use. Then, you simply click on the image to download it to your computer.

Here are 5 of my favorite sites:

1. PicJumbo, com
2. DeathToTheStockPhoto.com
3. Stockvault.net
4. Pixabay.com
5. FreeImages.com

Now that you have your images, how can you add that extra "punch" to them so they get some attention online? Let's look at...

6 sources to sharpen your visual marketing

Whoever said that looks don't matter has never hopped on the Internet. Social media may be powered by content, but it makes its mark through images and video. In order to make sure that your social media and blogging efforts are as effective as you'd like, you need to catch a visitor's eye as well as his or her mind. **Here's a statistic for you: visuals are processed an estimated 60,000 times faster in the brain than text! (http://blog.hubspot.com/marketing/visual-content-marketing-infographic)**

If you want to grab the casual, Internet visitor before he or she clicks away, you're likely going to do it through visuals.

Here are a few sites that can help:

QuotesCover.com

Are you a quote addict?

QuotesCover turns text into an eye-catching image so that you can impress your visitor with your visuals and your content. Even if you don't know anything about typography or composition, you can have a beautifully-designed quote to use on Facebook, Twitter or more with just a couple of clicks.

ReciteThis.com

Have you ever wanted to turn a quote into a masterpiece? It's easy with ReciteThis, which is similar to QuotesCover in terms of turning text into impressive visuals. ReciteThis pulls you in straight from the homepage, asking the tempting question: "Can I quote you?" Why, certainly!

PowToon.com

Sometimes words and visuals alone just aren't enough. PowToon goes that extra step to allow you to create animated videos and presentations – for free.

You can create website videos, product demonstrations, explainer videos and social clips, bringing a new dimension to your social-media profile.

PlaceIt.net

If you're looking to create eye-catching mockups and videos, PlaceIt is your place. You may have screenshots of your app, but how engaging is that? Answer: Not enough! With PlaceIt, you can process screenshots and come out with gorgeous, marketing collateral that will get your app where it needs to go – the top!

Canva.com

Canva is a great place to create social-media graphics from cover photos (to post images to ads). Their templates make it easy to create a branded graphic quickly!

PicMonkey.com

PicMonkey is my go-to place for editing, cropping and resizing photos. You can also create social-media graphics, edit with filters, text over photos, and so much more!

Here are some of our favorite mobile apps that will allow you to create graphics, edit photos and create video quickly and easily:

Text over photos:

- WordSwag
- Over
- Canva

Collages:

- Diptic
- PicPlayPost
- Layout

Video:

- Legend.Im
- Boomerang
- Flipagram

Printing:

- DesignShop

Editing:

- Camera+
- Prisma

Now you have some good tools for visuals. And this leads me to one of my favorite, social-media platforms. Let's cover Instagram!

Instagram

Instagram is one of the fastest-growing social networks and one of the best networks to connect with others to build your brand and to tell your story. Why? Photos and videos connect us to each other in a way that just doesn't happen with words or text. And with it's simplicity, Instagram has won over millions of loyal fans so...

How can you integrate Instagram into your social strategy?

1. Get creative – use other apps to add text over photos or create collages.
2. Add hashtags to each post – use three to five for each post.
3. Don't flood the feed – Space out your posts.
4. Respond to comments quickly.
5. Get artistic – Look for beauty and unique moments all around you.
6. Engage with hashtags – Search for relevant ones and like, comment or engage to build your community.
7. Tell your story – What gets you fired up everyday? Share that!

Did you know? 32% of internet users (28% of all U.S. adults) use Instagram (http://www.pewinternet.org/2016/11/11/social-media-update-2016/)

Top 5 tips to boost your Instagram engagement

Here comes the next question: How do you boost your own Instagram engagement ratio? The Forrester researchers offer a few suggestions.

1. Show me the human!

According to research done by the Georgia Institute of Technology and Yahoo Labs, Instagram photos featuring human faces are 38 percent more likely to get likes as well as 32 percent more likely to garner comments than their faceless counterparts. (https://www.yahoo.com/tech/want-to-get-more-likes-and-comments-on-instagram-show-80202758134.html)

2. Actual product use

Additionally, shots of real customers using products were the recipients of 30 percent more engagement. This increased when the posted pictures featured faces and product engagement.

3. Bleed bright and blue

Then there's the research conducted by the visual analytics platform Curalate, which after analyzing more than 8 million Instagram photos, found that pictures with blue as the dominant color received 24 percent more engagement than those with orange or red dominating. In addition, bright pictures got nearly a quarter more engagement than their darker counterparts. (http://www.curalate.com/blog/6-image-qualities-that-drive-more-instagram-likes)

4. Know when to post

When you're posting videos on Instagram, keep the clock in mind. Interestingly enough – some of the most ideal times are 2am and 5pm.)http://www.huffingtonpost.com/2015/02/25/get-instagram-likes_n_6751614.html) Also, according to the data, the most "engaged" time on Instagram changes from day to day: On Monday, for example, 5 p.m. is actually a pretty crummy time; engagement is highest at 7 p.m. and 10 p.m. On Friday, 1 a.m. and 8 p.m. are apparently the sweet spots

5. Hashtags are your friends

We found that engagement was particularly boosted by the presence of hashtags –especially when you can use three to five hashtags relevant to your content you are posting. By using hashtags, your Instagram content will be found by more people and result in more engagement.

Now, here are some of my favorite ways to maximize this hot, social-media platform…

5 ways to get intentional with Instagram:

As one of the fastest growing social-media-platforms, Instagram is also one of my favorites because:

- **It's still small.**

  Instagram is a great way to connect and get to know people better, because not "everyone" is on the platform.
- **It's clean and simple.**

  There are limited ads and no need for lists or filtering. It's one simple stream!

So how can you get intentional with Instagram, and make it make more sense for you and your business?

Here are five, simple tips you can implement immediately:

1. **Use hashtags**

   Hashtags are a simple way to broaden the audience who sees your Instagram posts. Tagstagram and TagForLikes are two simple apps that you can use to copy and paste popular hashtags into your post. *Pro tip:* Don't post all of your hashtags on the caption of your photo. This can make your photo look spammy. Post a caption, upload your photo and then add your captions in the comment section!

2. **Search for hashtags**

   As in all social networks, it's not just about pushing content and talking, but it's about engaging in your community. For example, if you are a Realtor in Denver, search the hashtag #denver or #movingtodenver. For a winery, popular hashtags may be #winetasting, #wineoclock or #winelover.

   See what appears and then like, comment and engage authentically. Be a helpful resource. *Pro tip:* Not sure which hashtags to search for? Brainstorm a list of five to ten keywords that people use when talking about your product or service.

3. **Look to your life as content**

Not sure what to post on Instagram? Look around you and see how you can showcase moments in your life including: moments of celebration with a client, moments with your family, moments on a great vacation, and more. I try to use Instagram as more than my camera roll on my iPhone and post an interesting vantage point or get creative with my photos. *Pro tip:* Try turning your camera a bit for a fun angle!

4. **Post consistently** Like any other, social network, make an effort to post consistently, at least a few times a week. When someone comes upon your profile and you haven't posted recently, it gives the impression that you aren't active on the network.

Pro tip: A few times a week, instead of uploading a photo to Facebook (as you may normally do), intentionally choose two or three to be posted on Instagram and then share them on Facebook. This kills two birds with one stone. It adds content to your Instagram feed but also allows you to use the photos on Facebook. Make sure you follow pro tip #1 above for using hashtags to ensure that you won't look spammy on Facebook.

5. **Engage authentically**

A few times a week, scroll through your Instagram feed and like and comment on photos from people you follow. Comment and like on photos that speak to you, that are funny, poignant or beautiful.

Pro tip: Don't click "like" on everything – authenticity is key!

And one other thing. Instagram video is heating up! Did you know you can take a video as you normally would with your smartphone and then import the clip?

You can also utilize fun apps like Pic Play Post to create collage photos in Instagram that are collages of photos AND video. The result is pretty amazing.

Advanced Instagram strategies

1. Put your phone in airplane mode to take pictures and filter.

By putting your phone in airplane mode, you can save your photos to your phone without having to publish on Instagram. This is a great feature if you want to take numerous photos and utilize the filters and other editing tools of Instagram without overwhelming your feed.

2. You can post from Instagram to Facebook OR you can post to Instagram and then wait to post to Facebook.

The benefit of doing this is that you can then change the caption for your Facebook posting. Why would you want to do this? Well, generally I like to include three or four hashtags with a photo when I post to Instagram.

Or, sometimes I'll mention that a "link is in my profile" when posting on Instagram. Both of these things don't translate well when posting automatically to Facebook. But by going back and editing the caption, I'm able to make the posting a bit more Facebook-friendly.

3. Create Instagram ads using Facebook Ad's Manager

Create Instagram ads using Facebook Ad's Manager. This hack is especially for those of you using social media for business. In the past, Instagram ads were only available to very large brands. But now, anyone can run an Instagram ad. To get started, visit Facebook.com/ads. You'll set these up very similar to Facebook ads, with options for targeting and setting your budget (you can spend as little as $5/day). It's definitely worth exploring if you're looking to expand your following!

Here are a few pro Instagram ad tips:

- Place ads in the app or at facebook.com/ads
- Run ads for 5-7 days
- **Pro tip:** run daytime or nighttime ads (i.e. showcase the home in the morning or in the evening)

4. Use Iconosquare.com for insight on the best time of day to post

What is the best time of day to post on Instagram? You can find this, and tons of other great-insights, using the free Iconosquare.com tool. This is an awesome tool to monitor your own Instagram engagement or, if you're a social-media consultant like me, this will help in creating reports for your clients.

5. Remember, life is content. Recognize the moments!

Take quality photos. The quality of your photos is going to play a big role in growing an Instagram following. I like to encourage my coaching clients to use their life as content, especially when it comes to Instagram. This is all about being aware of moments.

Also, be sure to take other steps to create better quality photos. Use natural light and the grid, and try shooting with different angles.

6. A great way to increase your Instagram engagement and following is to utilize the tag function

Tag, tag, tag – but do so strategically. A great way to increase your Instagram engagement and following is to utilize the tag function. Now, you don't want to overuse or misuse this to the point you are annoying people, but you do want to use it in a strategic and smart manner. Tag people (and brands) in both the photo and the comments. I find that you are more likely to get engagement when you tag in both places. You can also ask others to tag their friends. This is a great way to invite others into the conversation.

7. A great way to find hashtags is to do a search in Instagram with the category you are trying to target

Hashtag your way to success! We all know hashtags are huge for Instagram, but how do you pick the right ones? A great way to find hashtags is to do a search in Instagram with the category you are trying to target. See what the top hashtags are and use those. Ride the hashtag wave!

Here are a few hashtag tips for Instagram

- Use local and relevant hashtags up to 25
- Post them in the comments to not look "spammy" in the photo description
- Search your town to see trending Instagram hashtags
- Hashtags should reflect every part of the photo
  Example: #sf #sanfrancisco #sfhomes #sanfranciscohomes #realestate #realtors #lovewhereyoulive #thebay #bayarea #sfbayarea #instalove #instadaily #beautiful #homesforsale
- **Power tip:** write them in a Word doc and then copy/paste them when you post (or in a Note on your phone)

8. Use competitors to your advantage on Instagram

Utilize your competitors. If you're feeling stuck with Instagram or growing a following, try searching out your top three to five competitors or people who have a similar audience. Look who is liking their posts and follow some of those people.

And when you are using Instagram, don't forget Millennials. Connecting with Millennials on Instagram is one of the biggest reasons to embrace this platform.

How can you connect with millennials on Instagram?

Be consistent

When it comes to social media, no one likes a part-timer. If you're going to tackle Instagram, do it right and do it reliably. That means making a schedule and sticking to it. In other words, don't start off strong by posting three times-a-day and then go missing for two weeks. Remember that the more consistently you post, the more likely it is that Millennials will notice your brand and reward you with likes, comments and shares.

Use cultural relevance to your advantage

Nostalgia works beautifully if you can tap into the collective memories of Millennials. Moreover, content that is relevant to a particular time (be it then or now), or specific to a certain set of associations, will help Millennials make associations between your brand and treasured remembrances. Get them at their heart, and you'll see where they live.

Recognize the uniqueness of your millennial audience and make them feel special.

This can take the form of Instagram-only giveaways and contests or an exclusive sneak-peek at a new or emerging feature. The more you can make your millennial visitors feel seen and appreciated, the more they will want to reward your brand with their business.

Embrace the power of taggable posts

This is viral marketing at its most powerful. When one millennial guest tags another (or preferably, several), and the tagging goes from there, this is invaluable free-exposure for your brand or service. How can you beat that?

Originality is king

Millennials aren't coming to Instagram to see what they can see anywhere else on the internet. Instead, they expect that their favorite brands (and soon-to-be-favorites) are doing something unique and interesting on this popular-beyond-popular platform. Don't disappoint them! Instead, post something that will immediately engage followers and hopefully spur them to action.

How to leverage Instagram business profiles and Instagram stories

Are you maximizing Instagram business profiles and Instagram stories to build your brand, build sales, drive traffic to your website and build relationships? Here are a few things you need to know!

Why should you convert your personal profile to a business account on Instagram?

1. Robust analytics that are available
2. More ad options
3. Contact button – making it easier for people to reach you

How can you stay relevant with the Instagram algorithm?

- Post often 1-3 times a day
- Use 10-20 hashtags per post
- Engage with others: 5-10 people a day (like, comment)
- Post Instagram photos and use Instagram stories
- Place Instagram ads
- Post great content!

What is an Instagram story?

- Series of video clips (up to 10 seconds) or photos
- You can doodle, draw and write over each photo
- Use filters
- You can take a new photo or video or upload from your phone
- They disappear after 24 hours or you can download them to your phone to repurpose
- Why is this a big deal? Creating interactive, timely and relevant content quickly!

Think like a storyteller!

Have a beginning (what are you going to tell them), a middle with three, five or seven tips 3, 5 or 7 tips) and an end (with a call to action such as: where can they find you?)

Here is a calendar with 28 sample Instagram ideas for real estate:

Monday	Tuesday	Wednesday	Thursday	Friday	Saturday	Sunday
Local park	The reason why you do what you do	Best coffee shop in town	Broker open - doors	Local wine	Inspirational quote	Sunday open house - view
Happy clients at with their new keys	Broker open - views	Beautiful views	Best restaurant	Your team	Amazing doors	Summertime fun
Quote about real estate	Your car	Best happy hour	Happy clients at closing	Broker open – home details	Best kept secret in my town	Fun with clients and friends
Thing you love most about your home	Market stats	What home means to you	Before and after pics	Your 3 fave people	Gorgeous home details	Keeping busy

Now, speaking of Instagram and visuals, how about Pinterest?

According to Pew Research, in 2016, roughly three-in-ten online Americans (31%) use Pinterest, identical to the 31% who used the platform in 2015. (http://www.pewinternet.org/2016/11/11/social-media-update-2016/)

If you're not taking advantage of this, then you're leaving good business on the table.

Of course, therein lies the question. How do you make Pinterest work best for you? I've gathered a few suggestions for best practices…

To start, it's crucial that your Pinterest boards be as user-friendly as possible. Make sure they're optimized by naming them properly and classifying them in an easy-to-understand way. The best method of doing this is creating multiple boards to cluster relevant content together. At the same time, ensure that your pins are optimized too.

And when uploading your own pins, make sure they're the ideal size for the platform.

Also, consider utilizing online resources to easily enhance your photos. A few of my favorites include:

- PicMonkey
- Canva
- GetStencil.com

Remember, pinning frequency is important. This means striking a balance between pinning too little and too much. How will you know the right amount? Well, make sure that you don't go an extended period of time without any post. Be consistent, but avoid mass posting in one fell swoop, or you risk pushing away your followers. And you may want to consider scheduling pins, a feature available on Buffer or Tailwind.

Also, take advantage of Rich Pins. When Pinterest first was created in 2010, you could only use one type of pin, but that's the bad old days. Today, there are six different types of Rich Pins that will allow you to provide more information: Place, Article, Product, Recipe, Movie and App.

Particularly helpful are the Article pins, which offer your headline, author and story description. Product pins help e-commerce firms provide availability and pricing along with letting audience members know where products can be purchased.

Finally, remember that it's easy to measure your marketing efforts through Pinterest's web-analytics tool. Keep a finger on the pulse of what's working and ditch what's not. Staying flexible and paying attention to what's garnering the most results will particularly help you rock the power of Pinterest!

How to use Pinterest to curate content for Facebook

At a loss as to what to post on your Facebook business page? Did you know that <u>Pinterest</u> is one of the best methods to curate your content to post to your Facebook page? At its essence, Pinterest is made up of buckets of content that can be repurposed for your Facebook page.

For example, if you're a real estate agent in San Francisco, your Pinterest boards may look like this:

- Only in SF
- San Francisco Living
- San Francisco Dining
- San Francisco Sunsets
- Our Awesome Team
- San Francisco Style

Pinterest users create these boards by re-pinning other photos or installing the "Pin It" button and pinning things from their own sites or favorite sites they visit daily. You may pin things to these boards from local sites like SFgate.com or 7×7.com.

Think about what buckets of content you would like to share on Facebook. If part of your strategy is to post one piece of content from each bucket every day, it really takes the guesswork out of what to post. Think of each bucket of content as a theme for your Facebook page.

For example, here's a sample Facebook content strategy if you are in real estate:

- **Monday:** Post a fun, San Francisco photo.
- **Tuesday:** Post one photo of an amazing home – perhaps, one of your current or past listings.
- **Wednesday**: Post a photo of one of the best places to eat in the city with a link back to the restaurant.
- **Thursday:** Post an incredible, sunset photo.
- **Friday:** Post a photo with a little-known fact about your team.

When adding the content to Facebook from Pinterest, it's recommended you include a link back to where someone can "pin it" to read later.

Visual content is one of the best ways to boost your engagement on Facebook. And I think you'll be surprised at what Pinterest content can do for your news feed so here are some…

Advanced Pinterest tips

Pinterest is an aspirational platform where people go to dream about their new home, their upcoming wedding, the party they are going to plan, and more. There are a lot of social networks available to help you connect with people, build relationships and show off your business, but Pinterest – with its emphasis on big images, ease of sharing, and a reputation for planning your dreams – is perfect for many types of businesses.

Here are a few advanced tips when it comes to Pinterest:

1. Maximize image height

Pinterest is one of the most visual social-channels, and content is arranged in long columns. This means that you get the most space on a screen if you have tall images.

You can sometimes accomplish this by cropping your pictures into an exaggerated portrait orientation, but you don't want to lost half of the picture, either. A better option is to collage several pictures together into a column. There are several websites – like <u>PicMonkey</u> and <u>Fotor</u> – that will let you up-load and collage pictures for free.

2. Build links

As often as possible, but only where it makes sense to do so, link your pins back to your website or blog. There are two ways to do this. You can link the image and type a link in the description.

If you repin something, or you pin something from the web, Pinterest will automatically link the image to the page it came from. If you upload a pin from your computer, you can still link the image by clicking the Edit icon once you've saved your pin, and typing it in manually.

The second option is typing a link into the description of your pin. This is a better way to build links if the image isn't yours.

3. Create a wide-range of boards

Put together Pinterest boards on a wide range of relevant topics. Here are some of the most popular types of boards you can create:

- Home
- Beauty
- Fashion
- Art
- Tech
- Parenting
- Travel
- Fashion
- Food
- Fitness
- Gardening

4. Create "pin it for later" links

When you share a blog post to social media, you can give people the options to "Pin the post for later read."

Here's how:

- After publishing a new blog, you can pin an image from the new blog post.
- Copy the link for the Pin.
- Share this link with the blog post as a way to "Pin it for later."

The main idea is that people will add your pin to one of their Pinterest boards and back to your content later when they want to read and engage. It's a great way to allow others to bookmark your content for later reading.

Hopefully, you have a better understanding of using visuals, Instagram and Pinterest in your social-media efforts.

Let's take a closer look at Facebook...

Chapter 12

• • •

Facebook Business Pages and Facebook Ads

Facebook Business Page basics

This is an important component of your social media strategy, and it can be all about business, marketing listings, data, and so forth. But you want to proceed with caution here... it does take a lot of time, effort and strategy, and these days, even a little bit of money for Facebook advertising.

I'll go out on a limb and say that Facebook Business Pages are not for everyone. However, if you have the time, the money and the strategy already in place, you may want to move forward. It all depends on what works best for you.

5 ways to start building business today with your Facebook page

1. Set up your Page

It needs to be prepared in a way that's going to be a compelling, online hub for your business endeavors. Go to facebook.com/pages to set up your business Page for free.

Remember that a Facebook Page allows potential clients to discover you when searching. Plus, it makes you connected and ready to have conversations with that clientele, whether they are individuals or through a larger debate in a post. Make your Page easy to find by requesting a relevant, web address. Also, ensure that your contact information is posted with your business address, phone number, email, and website. If you have set up your Page already – make sure you check to make sure your About section on your Facebook Page is up-to-date.

2. Who is your audience?

Figure out whom you're targeting through this effort. Here are a few questions to ask yourself in order to narrow this down:

- What are the demographics of your ideal customer? For example, what is their age range and geographic region?
- What type of outreach will best suit this audience? Are they more likely to respond to specific messages, services, products, or a well-targeted sales offer?
- What are the commonalities between your desired customers?
- What can your business provide these people?
- Who can you tell about your Page? Don't forget to encourage your current supporters and clientele to like your Page, and they'll spread the word!

3. Engage your audience with a thoughtful presentation

This starts with personalizing your Page with a profile picture and cover photo so that your fans have a visual representation to connect with your business. Think in terms of telling your story. This also applies to the content you add. Use milestones and key moments to create trust on your Page. People want to know more about your business, including its history. Consider filling in your Timeline to post milestones about your company. Also, make sure you have a branded cover photo which you can create for free using Canva.com or PicMonkey.com.

4. Use quality content to engage your audience and keep them coming back

Here are a few ways to do that:

- **Post regularly and in a timely manner.**

  People want to know you're here to stay. Be consistent and you'll not only retain your current fans, but attract new ones too. Use the scheduling tool available on Facebook business pages to schedule content in advance. Don't set it and forget it, and don't automate everything, but taking the time once a week to schedule content for the next 3-5 days allows for consistency.

- **Timeliness when it comes to interaction is also key.**

  If one of your fans has a question or comment, be sure to address that without letting too much time slip by. Use the Facebook Pages Manager mobile app to monitor notifications and respond in a timely manner.

- **Be authentic.**

  Your fans want to know who you are and what you stand for. Be yourself, and people will respond positively. If you have a team or others posting or scheduling content for your business page, it's vital that they understand your brand voice so that your posts sound as authentic as possible. Pro tip: If you are thinking of hiring someone to manage your Facebook business page, ask them to write 5-10 sample posts on a Word or Google document. This is a great way to judge their writing skills, creativity and how well they understand your business and voice.

- **Boost popular posts**.

  If you're getting a lot of traction on a particular post, don't keep it to yourself. Make sure others know about it as well. View your Facebook Insights weekly to see which posts gain the highest engagement (like, clicks, shares and comments) and then post most of those. For posts related to your business, I highly recommend boosting those posts by $5-10 at a minimum – depending on your budget. For example, I would not boost a post that linked to another website or news site, but if I posted a photo of myself with a client or posted a link to one of my blog posts, I would boost that to have it be seen in front of more people. The best bang for your buck when it comes to boosting post is typically to boost to people who like your page and/or their friends. Remember, Facebook severely limits who sees your post, so boosting can help tremendously.

5. Pinpoint and promote

Use Facebook Ads Manager (https://www.facebook.com/ads/manager/) and created targeted ads that will attract your ideal clientele with well-honed messages. Ask yourself questions similar to when you were targeting your ideal audience. Who are you seeking and how are you going to reach them? Facebook Insights let you hone in on what's working and eliminate what's not.

And going along with this information, here are...

5 simple ways to improve your status updates on your Facebook Business Page

Facebook status updates are a powerful way to convey your message in a concise, personal and viral manner. You may already be harnessing this opportunity, but chances are that you can make your message stand out even more strongly.

1. Keep it brief

While Facebook differs from Twitter in that you're not constrained to a small number of characters, your audience's preferences may well prove to be that limiting factor.

However your readers may be viewing your updates though, it's likely that they're going to respond more positively to something on the shorter side – say 250 characters or less. Toward this end, don't try to tackle too much in a single update. It's better to concentrate on one subject at a time and successfully get your message across.

2. Stash the stuffy

Facebook is a personal platform. You're going to turn off your fans if you choose to talk to them in too formal of a tone. Instead, aim for a professional, yet informal, voice where you speak directly to your audience. For example, say "you" rather than "my clientele" in your posts. Your fans want to feel as though they know you. Don't let your tone get in the way of that.

Incorporate visuals and videos that are eye-catching and relevant, and use themed days to help plan your status updates. For example, Tuesday, could be #TipTuesday or Wednesday could be #WineWednesday. Don't overdo the hashtags, but by having a consistent theme a couple times a week, it makes it easier to plan. And, it's something your fans will come to expect!

3. Use the Facebook Like button

If you're adding a link to your update, consider using a Facebook Like button on the external post (on your website). While links in status updates can be helpful when it comes to driving readers to your website or another external page, they may not be so effective if you're looking to increase your Like count.

This is because people may jet off to the external link and forget to come back to like the original post. One way you can help fight this is to add a Facebook Like button to your blog post. This allows readers to like the post directly from your site itself.

If you're including external links in your Facebook status update, consider adding a Facebook Like button to your original post.

4. Ask questions

Increase your engagement by asking a relevant question in your status update. However, keep in mind that questions placed at the end of a post are far more likely to get your audience talking.

Good words to use include *when, where* and *would*. Avoid "why" questions as these garner the lowest amount of comments and likes. One thing to note is that this strategy is usually most effective after you have more than 1,000 likes. There is nothing worse then asking a question and no one answers it so although questions are a great strategy, wait until you build up your likes first.

5. Offer resources

In order to position yourself as an authority, not only on Facebook but in your industry, it's helpful to provide advice and suggestions that will help your readers achieve their goals and come up with a slew of new ideas and visions.

Using your status update for this purpose is a simple and powerful way to show your readership that you are a person in-the-know. What can you offer? Try eBooks, white papers, how-to guides, checklists and more!

Should you open your Facebook Page to ratings and reviews?

People trust other peoples' assessments of businesses. That's why it can be a very powerful tool to have ratings and reviews on your Facebook page. And it's easy to do this. In fact, just by taking a few steps, you're well on your way to widely promoting your brand even more.

First off, you need to categorize your page as a Local Business. In addition, you'll need to add your business address to your page. Page categories may be chosen when you create a page or by changing your page's category after it is already created.

Should you later change your page's address, you will still keep your existing ratings and/or reviews.

Now that you have ratings and reviews set up, there are two key things left to do:

1. **Promote it!**
   The Reviews tab is now a unique link that you can promote via your email list or other social networks as a way for people to review you. You can also email it to select customers or clients one-on-one and ask for reviews. Imagine reaching out to five people a week!
2. **Respond to all reviews quickly.**
   Respond quickly by clicking "like" or leaving a comment...make sure you acknowledge them!

Once you start responding and posting, you may start to ask yourself...

Are you posting too frequently on Facebook?

Many people neglect to post frequently enough when establishing a professional or personal Facebook page, but what about those who post far too frequently?

If you post too often, you may annoy followers by choking up their News Feed. No matter how interesting and fascinating you are (and of course you are!), posting more frequently than desirable will lead to people unfollowing you, and you certainly don't want that.

We have found that most engagement on a status update, or any other type of post, will take place within the first five hours after it has posted.

What does that mean? Perhaps you should wait at least that amount of time before posting again, so you don't overwhelm your audience.

However, you should post each day. Failing to do so means that you're falling out of the minds of your audience, and you didn't create a Facebook page only to be forgotten!

When you're posting, here are a few key things to remember:

- **Each post should be high-quality**

  Don't post simply for the sake of posting. Instead, post because it's interesting and relevant to the audience members who are going to be reading, and hopefully responding to, it. Each post may be considered a call-to-action in a sense, since what you're trying to do is connect with your followers and ultimately entice them to use your services.

- **Facebook Insights can give you the information you need**

  Different strategies may bring different results so you might want to play around and then look at the results you're getting. Say, for example, three updates per day is getting a good amount of reach, but four is resulting in unlikes. This means three-a-day and no more is a good idea.

- **You may get feedback in the form of messages from your audience**

  If you're hearing that your posts are becoming tiresome, then you know what to do – dial it back! Another way to measure this is by the amount of response you're receiving on posts. If you get more likes and comments with fewer posts, then you might assume that this smaller number is your sweet spot for posting.

Other peoples' opinions are also a great way to get feedback on whether your posts are excessive. Talk to those who know and share your goals. They will likely be honest and give you good feedback that will help you fine-tune what you're doing and how you're doing it.

Keep this in mind... striking the right balance takes time and effort. You're going to want to work somewhat quickly here, though. Internet time isn't exactly like offline time. It works more quickly with less patience. If people feel as though you're wasting their time with too much information, they may ditch you very quickly – and you don't want that. Instead, you want an engaged audience that's happy with the amount of information they're receiving and neither wants more or less.

Scheduling posts to your Facebook Business Page

There is one thing I get asked about all the time: "How can I stay on top of posting consistently to my Facebook Business Page?"

The answer? Easy. You can schedule content.

Here are a few important do's and don't for scheduling Facebook posts to your business page:

Do's:

- **Plan**

  Plan one day a week where you will schedule some of your content. Set aside an hour or so to organize your thoughts and decide what you are going to post over the next three to five days.

- **Insights**

  Check out Facebook Insights to see what time of day people who like your page are most active on Facebook and most likely to interact with your content.

- **Be creative**

  Your content can be questions you ask on your Page, links to articles, images you create, or video links.

Don'ts

- **Over-schedule**

  Don't schedule content too far in advance or rely just on scheduled content. Make sure you fill in throughout the week with content that is "off the cuff" and unplanned!

- **Variety**

  Don't just schedule one type of content. Mix it up and have fun.

- **Over curate**

  Don't just post curated content from other sources, make some of the content you post your own.

On a side note, I prefer to schedule directly using Facebook's platform versus using a third-party application. I find it receives the best engagement this way. Also, it's important to note that you can always edit or delete scheduled content if needed. Lastly, you can't use this Facebook scheduling tool for your personal Facebook profile, only your Business Page.

And now that you have your scheduling down, how do you increase engagement?

5 quick tips to increase engagement on your Facebook Business Pages

People do business with people they know, like and trust. Facebook is one of the best tools available to build relationships, get to know people and build trust. One of the ways you do that on Facebook is by posting engaging content.

Remember when the only information you had about a potential client was their name, phone number and perhaps email? Now, the culture of sharing has changed; people openly share about their interests, vacations, family, and more. Because of Facebook, it is easier now than ever to build relationships and engage with potential clients over the long-haul.

Here are five, quick-and-easy tips to increase engagement on your Facebook Business Pages:

1. **Stay relevant**

   Timing is everything. Are you posting a message at 7 a.m. about dinnertime? Or, are you posting during the summer about a snow day? Stay relevant with your content by keeping in mind when people will see your content. Staying topical will keep people's attention and engage them more in your content.

2. **Include humor**

   Sometimes we take ourselves so seriously. Make sure you incorporate some fun into your posts on Facebook. Pinterest is a great source for fun quotes and photos that you can share on Facebook. Keeping it light makes it fun, and it is an easy way to build engagement.

3. **Brief is better.**

    We found that posts that are between 100 and 250 characters (less than 3 lines of text) see about 60% more likes, comments and shares than posts greater than 250 characters. Keep it short and edit ruthlessly!

4. **Don't post too often.**

    With our clients, we have found that a Facebook post on a Business Page "lives" about three hours. The biggest mistake I see people making with their Facebook Business Page is posting too often. This is why having a content strategy is key. Know when and what you will post.

5. **Photos (and videos) are still king**

    Photos (and video; live and recorded) are undeniably still the king of engagement on Facebook. Posts including a picture generate about 120% more engagement. Be smart about your photos. Are you pinning interesting photos? Use some of those photos in your Facebook content strategy.

Now that you've created a Facebook Business Page, you're going to want to get the most out of it. While your own mileage will vary in terms of how you go out to accomplish this, I've pulled together several suggestions that I think will be helpful to you no matter what your individual goals might be.

Taking your business Page to the next level

Boosting your page

Boosting your Business Page's activity often begins with those who are already interested in and engaging with it. Tap into the collective power of your current fan-base and ask them to like and share your content. Do this directly, honestly and not too terribly often, and you'll reap the benefits without causing undue resentment.

Cross-promoting your page

Cross-promotion can be a gold mine if you're looking to light a fire under your Page. This can be accomplished in a few different ways, and you can use one, or both, depending on what works for you.

First, consider joining forces with other page managers who work in a similar industry to yours. This enables you to tap into each other's clientele and create a potentially valuable working relationship.

Second, your cross-promotion can also take the form of creating a presence on fan pages that you might find within your professional niche. This helps you develop authority as you offer comments and useful information. Just be sure to post as your own page rather than your personal profile so your business gets the credit.

Mobile first

Mobile-phone users are making up an ever-greater percentage of your on-line audience, so don't forget to take them into consideration when posting. This means fewer words and more images to draw in restless cell-phone scrollers.

Facebook Offers

Once you have hit 400 Likes on your Page, you'll be able to access Facebook Offers. This allows you to provide interactive offers that can not only be redeemed by customers either online or in-person, but that can hopefully go viral in order to gain you more notoriety and business. Remember to accompany the offer with some catchy visuals to really pull people in!

Video is king.

Uploading video directly to your Facebook page (as opposed to a link to YouTube, Vimeo, etc.) will add an entire, new dimension to your page. Facebook's algorithm appears to love organic videos - and so will your fans!

Go live!

Facebook Live is one of the hottest features. With the push of a button, you can go live on your Facebook Business Page, personal profile or even within a group. The longer you can stay on live, the higher your engagement rate tends to go. What a great way to connect with your audience – live and in real time! Plus, that live video stays on your profile after you stop broadcasting so people can still watch the replay afterward!

Now that we've talked about Facebook Pages. Let's dig into Facebook Advertising.

I have spent a ridiculous amount of time and money on advertising in this space. I've learned quite a bit over the years through my own trial-and-error as well as working with many different companies, both large and small, on their paid Facebook marketing. I'd love to share a few of my biggest tips with you.

Here are a few things to note in getting started with Facebook ads.

Utilize targeting through Facebook's ad platform.

A lot of times when people get started with Facebook ads, they start by boosting a post. While that's certainly not a bad place to start, I think the biggest opportunity for people is to go to Facebook's ad platform at facebook.com/ads or their Power Editor and use their targeting tool.

The reason I say this is because the targeting with boosting a post is pretty limited. But when you're using the ad platform, you can target many things including age, gender, zip codes, income, net worth, millennials, people who have kids at home, people on their birthdays, people who have iPhones, etc. The amount of targeting you can do through this platform is robust!

Use Facebook Insights to hone your ad targeting.

Look at your Facebook Insights to see statistics on your target market. Use this knowledge to improve your ad targeting. For even more in depth information, try the Audience Insights tool where you can get some amazing information on people you are already connected to on Facebook.

Create a custom audience.

If you are doing any sort of email marketing, you can actually download your database and then upload it to Facebook so it becomes a custom audience. The benefit of doing this is that you can run ads that are just targeting people who already know you. This is huge. One of the ways we get people to buy from us is the know, like and trust factor. So if people already know, like and trust you enough to be on your email marketing list, running ads seen only by these people will be highly effective.

You can also create look-a-like audiences based on custom audiences or Pages that you are an admin for. Basically, Facebook can create a custom audience for you that looks similar to other audiences that are in your demographic.

Use Facebook's pixel.

This may sound complicated, but it's actually really easy. When you go to Facebook.com/ads you can create what's called a custom pixel. Basically, you push a button and Facebook is going to shoot back to you this long piece of code. Then, all you need to do is copy and paste that code into your website.

If you have a WordPress site, it's very easy to do. If you work with a webmaster or someone else who manages your website, simply email them the code and have them drop it into your website.

The benefit of this is when you have the Facebook pixel on your website, every time someone goes to your website, and then goes back to Facebook, they will potentially see your ads. This is a small thing that can make a really big difference. Just like any other marketing, the more people see you the more likely they are to contact and work with you. If you have ever been shopping on Amazon and looked at a pair of shoes and didn't buy them, but then when you went to Facebook, and that pair of shoes started following you on Facebook – you've been retargeted.

Split test.

Split-testing is something I do almost every time I run a Facebook ad. This is basically running the same ad/offer only you change out the text, the headline and/or the image. Generally speaking, every time I run an ad, I try to split test five to seven, different versions of that ad. My personal, favorite method is to keep the text the same and change out the image. The beauty of split-testing is that it allows you to really see what is working.

Target your ideal audience.

Using tools like custom audiences, retargeting and look-a-like audiences will allow you to target exactly who you want to target and your ideal audience. Pro tip: use a landing page platform like leadpages.net to easily capture leads on Facebook ads.

One thing to remember, with Facebook advertising, only 20% of your image can be text.

Create powerful images for your Facebook ads.

Images are everything. As we all know, a picture is worth a thousand words (and a video, even more!) Especially on Facebook, images and video are huge. Canva.com is a great tool for creating branded images for ads. Organically-uploaded videos to Facebook can work really well for your brand.

The biggest thing with Facebook ads is to experiment. You want to test what works and what doesn't work. And of course, things are always changing. Don't be afraid to spend $5-$10, and try something out.

Optimize your Facebook Ads with these crucial steps:

- **Identify your goal(s)**
  Right out of the gate, you'll want to figure out why you're working with Facebook Ads and what it is you wish to achieve. Facebook will actually ask you this question before you start creating your ad, so it serves you well to understand what you want to do beforehand.
- **Separate mobile and desktop ads**
  Proper ad optimization means using separate ad-sets for these types of calls-to-action so that you can make each as appropriate as possible for a given device (for example, mobile phones, tablets, desktop computers, etc.).
- **Divide your audience into more manageable-segments**
  Identifying your correct target-audience is key to reaching the right people. Break up potential audiences into smaller groups, and then run simultaneous campaigns to see which one gains the most traction.
- **Select the right call to action**
  Facebook will ask you to do this while you're setting up your ads. Go to the Ad Setup menu to choose your call-to-action, and keep in mind that these will have a major impact on your conversion and click-through rates – so choose carefully.
- **Keep track of the right performance metrics**
  A vital metric here is the average value-per-customer minus the cost-per-customer. Also, if you're looking to get more Likes through your Facebook Ads campaign, focus on cost-per-like.
- **Keep it short, sweet and simple**
  The fewer the characters in the Facebook Ad, the higher the possibility for engagement. This closely follows typical metrics in Facebook's News Feed. When working with text, use a strong

statement, question or call-to-action. This spurs a response on the part of the reader. Often times the best text includes this formula:

- Question about a pain point
- How you can help
- Call to action

For example, your ad may read like this: "Worried about moving? I can help. Check out my free cheat-sheet with 10 helpful tips today!

- **Experiment with different images**

  This is the most important part of your Facebook Ad, and it will determine whether or not your audience clicks through to read your content. Play around to identify what works best for you.

- **Schedule and rotate ads.**

  Keep the boredom factor in mind here. In order to not only reach the maximum audience, but to keep that audience from tuning out, you're going to want to change your ads regularly. In addition, it's important to schedule ads so that you have a predictable way of knowing who you're reaching and when you're reaching them.

10 ways to maximize Facebook ad images

Advertising online means having to pay attention to the visuals. This is particularly true with Facebook Ads. Here, there is so much competition for a potential client's attention that it bears taking some time to make sure your images are the ones that grab eyes.

With this in mind, let's look at a few ways to get the most out of your Facebook Ad images. Here are some tips from Facebook itself:

1. **The images in your ad should appear natural and appropriate for a viewer's News Feed.** To achieve this, try depicting people using your product rather than just the product itself. It's more engaging to show a person using a product than just the product on its own.

2. **Limit your image to less than 20 percent text.** This is because text-heavy images can be read as spam and then ignored. You can use Facebook's own grid tool to check this percentage. The Facebook Grid Tool will help you make sure your ad's image encompasses less than 20 percent text.

3. **Crop tightly around the most essential part of the image in order to focus your message.** Smart cropping helps your audience focus on your core message.

4. **Bright colors grab people's attention!**

5. **High-resolution images are optimal.** You can use Shutterstock photos that Facebook has available for advertisers or can download other great stock-photos from sites like Pixabay, Death to Stock Photo or Unsplash. You can also create great graphics with Photoshop or Canva.

6. **Don't forget about your brand image.** Your brand's character and unique personality should be represented by your image including fonts, colors and logos as needed.

7. **Simple is solid.** People have short, attention spans online. Embrace this. Don't fight it. Sometimes the best ads only have a few words. Less is more!

8. **Think in terms of benefits.** Your image should represent what your product can do for customers. Does your image display what you can offer?

9. **Less than 90 characters of text is ideal.** You don't want your message getting cut-off on smaller screens.

10. **Target your ideal audience.** Create different ads to capture as many people as possible.

Chapter 13

• • •

How to Create a Smart Facebook Strategy on a Budget

We know Facebook is important, but for many business owners, budget is top of mind. So, how can you generate more engagement, more traffic to your website – and ultimately more business on Facebook without spending a ton of money?

First off, Facebook never replaces what is already working in your business – it only can make it better (when done right!)

There are a number of ways you can maximize Facebook on a budget – here are a few of the most important tips and strategies you can implement today.

1. **Think beyond the now.** The biggest challenge with most business owners and real estate professionals is content and thinking ahead in terms of content. I recommend using a content grid to think about the type of content you could create or curate based on your brand. (See the chapter on content strategy for more on this!)

A content grid is a simple spreadsheet where you map out the 30 or so topics that are related to who you are, your brand and your expertise. (Note: You can download the complete content grid at KatieLance.com/ContentGrid)

2. **Batch your content.** In addition to planning ahead with a content grid, one of the best things you can do to be consistent with your page is to use Facebook's scheduling tool. By 'batching your content' – meaning scheduling out 5-7 days at a time – you will ensure that you have consistent content on your site.

Know the best time to post to your Page. Use the Insights tab on your Facebook Page to schedule content at the optimal time for when your fans are most likely to be on Facebook and then schedule out your content.

I recommend scheduling content 5-7 days in advance – nothing more than that. Also, you need to have a system in place for responding quickly to messages and comments.

3. **Have a system for responding quickly.** Download the Facebook Pages app (available for iOS and Android) and then make sure your notifications are set to 'ON' – this way, anytime someone reaches out to you on your Page, you will receive that right away.
4. **Boost your posts on a budget.** One of the best ways to get your content in front of more people is to boost your posts. Only boost posts that are linking back to your site. Why? No need to drive traffic

anywhere else right? This is why it's ideal if some or all of the posts on your Facebook Page link back to your site or your blog.

Start with boosting your posts by $5-10 each to people who like your page and their friends. By boosting the post to people who like your page and their friends – they are more likely to click on the post. You can run targeting on a boosted post – but to get the most bang for your buck when boosting – you want to boost to people who already know, like and trust you!

5. **Get more life out of past posts by boosting!** Extend the life of your posts. Go back to your Insights tab, click Posts and then sort by Engagement. Here, you will see the posts that got the most engagement on your Page. You can then choose to boost any one of those posts. If those posts are still relevant, pick 3-5 and boost each by $5-10 each to generate more traffic and engagement to your page.

6. **Get the most of each post by tagging.** Did you know there is a simple 'hack' to bring more people into each of your posts? When you post something on your business page that you think may also appeal to one of your Facebook friends you can click the drop-down arrow on your post and comment as yourself versus your page – then, you can tag any friends who you think may be interested in this post. Be careful here – don't spam your friends but tag a handful of friends. This will bring them to the post to hopefully like or comment – which will help get your post seen by more people!

7. **Promote your Page through email.** There are two simple things you can do to promote your Page through email. First, make sure you have your Facebook Page link easily listed in your email signature – I love using WiseStamp for this!

Secondly, make it a point in your email marketing efforts to promote your Facebook Page from time to time. For example, if you are emailing your sphere once a month using Mailchimp, Aweber, Constant Contact or any other email marketing system – make sure you not only put a link into your newsletter to promote your Page, but you give people a reason why they should like or visit your page. For example, you may say, "Are we connected yet on Facebook? Visit and like my business page this month to stay in the know about the latest homes going on the market in your area and selling in your neighborhood!"

8. **Promote your Page on all of your blog and/or videos.** At the end of each blog post and/or video – make sure to add a simple CTA (call to action) – something as simple as, "I'd love your thoughts on this too – leave me a comment on my Facebook Page which is_____"

9. **Invite people who like your posts to like your page.** This is one of my very favorite Facebook business page hacks. Here's how it works – if you receive more than a few likes on a post, you can click on the list of people who liked the post and are then given the option to invite them to like your page. This little hack has been a huge tool for increasing Facebook likes for both my clients and myself. This is now something I do about once a week and it's helped me consistently increase my Facebook likes.

10. **Create and upload video to your business Page.** One of the best ways to drive traffic to your Facebook Page and generate business from it is to create simple videos that are uploaded directly into Facebook. When you upload video directly into Facebook, you will see a big jump in organic (non-paid) reach and engagement.

If you've never done video before, I encourage you to think about creating short videos giving tips and answering questions. If you get asked a question more than once, it's a great opportunity to create a quick video. When you create your video, make sure you follow the simple rule: tell them who you are and what you are going to tell them, tell them what you are going to tell them and then wrap it up with a simple call-to- action with where they can connect with you.

A great place to start with video is by doing a Facebook Live video, where you are live broadcasting to people who like your page. You can access Facebook Live through the Facebook Pages Manager mobile app.

11. **A picture is worth a thousand words.** Pictures and visuals are still one of the number one things you can add to your Facebook Business Page. You can create simple graphics that are branded to your Page using tools like Canva.com or PicMonkey.com. Create graphics such as 'before and after' photos of homes, photos that represent the community you live in, inspirational or funny quotes, and/or photos of you and your happy clients.

Creating a Facebook strategy on a shoestring budget is possible. The key is getting a few systems in place for creating and posting content as well as making it a priority on your schedule.

The key to anything is time and although it doesn't take a lot of money to have a successful business page – time is money and it's the only thing we have! Schedule time each week to plan and schedule your content as well as create content. You may also look into hiring a Virtual Assistant and/or Copywriter on a part-time or project basis to assist you with some of these tasks.

Chapter 14

●　●　●

The Biggest Mistakes Business Owners are Making on Facebook

As a social media strategist who has worked with hundreds of business owners over the years, I've found that there are some common mistakes that I see people making over and over again. In no particular order, here's a list of the biggest mistakes business owners are making on Facebook.

Mistake 1 on Facebook: too many hashtags. I see this one all of the time. An individual or business page will post on Facebook and mistake the platform with Twitter or Instagram. Hashtags work really well on Twitter and Instagram but don't necessarily work very well on Facebook.

Mistake 2 on Facebook: automating posts from one platform to another. I realize people are trying to save time by pushing their posts from other platforms (Twitter or Instagram) to Facebook - but it just doesn't come across well. Be sure to treat each platform separately and post accordingly.

Mistake 3 on Facebook: too long of a post. Now, I understand there's a time and a place for the occasional longer post but in general, it's a mistake to constantly post lengthy posts. People just simply won't read them. People want things that are quick, easy and fast to digest. Keep in mind that 89% of Facebook users are on a mobile device. Aim to keep your posts short and sweet.

Mistake 4 on Facebook: sharing your Facebook account with your spouse. If you're a business owner, do not share your Facebook account with your spouse. I see this often and it just looks very unprofessional. For example, your Facebook account should not be "Joe 'N Susie Smith" - have separate accounts. Even if you aren't going to accept every friend request - when you are in a leadership position, having an account shared with your spouse gives the wrong perception.

Mistake 5 on Facebook: adding your job title to your Facebook personal profile name. Don't add your job title onto your personal profile name. I see this especially in the real estate industry. While I understand why people do this, please know you don't have to add the title Realtor for people to know that you're in real estate. So, instead of being "Betty Jones Realtor" - just be "Betty Jones" and then make sure in your About Section you add in your title and brokerage.

Mistake 6 on Facebook: not making it easy for prospects to find you. You're not making it easy for people to find you. You want to make it really easy for people to find you. What I mean by this is on your personal profile you should include where you live, where you work and your contact information. This doesn't mean you have to have your cell phone number listed, but you should at minimum include your email or your website. This is critical if you have a common name. If I am specifically looking for a "Joe Johnson" I will probably find hundreds of results - but by adding in location, job and title - it makes it much easier for me to find you.

Make it easy for people to contact you by including your information in your personal profile.

Mistake 7 on Facebook: having a profile photo that does not look like you. You have to have a profile photo that looks like you. Don't use a photo that is outdated. People should easily be able to recognize you from your photo. Also, it's best to use a photo that is just of you versus your entire family. Save the family photo for your cover photo.

Mistake 8 on Facebook: don't be polarizing. My advice is there's a fine line between being your authentic self and sharing your viewpoints and opinions...and polarizing other people. It's one thing to be passionate about your beliefs, but in this day and age with social media there are many blurred lines between personal and professional. It's important to remember that what you put out there sticks with you for a long time - your digital legacy.

Mistake 9 on Facebook: not checking your notifications. This may seem like a simple no-brainer, but I see a lot of business owners that just get too busy and forget to check their notifications. With Facebook, you can't just set it and forget it. Responding is just as important, if not more important, than what you post on Facebook.

Mistake 10 on Facebook: outsourcing too much of your personal social media. I often hear from business owners that they just don't have time for social media. I'm a firm believer that social media does not have to take a lot of time, especially if you have a strategy in place. Now, it's fine to outsource certain aspects of your social media - but don't outsource the relationships.

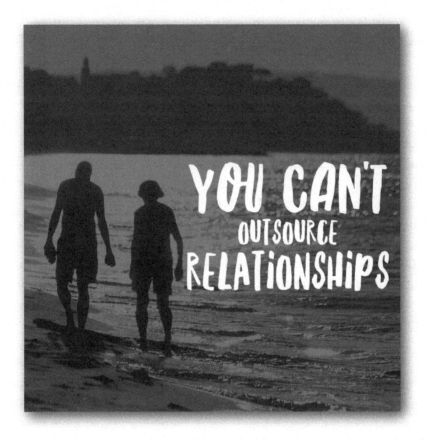

You may choose to outsource things like blog post creation, graphic design and scheduling some content - but what you can't outsource is the value you bring to commenting and engaging with your friends, colleagues and clients in an authentic way. Think of it as a big dinner party; if you had a dinner party with your 10 most important clients - would you have your assistant be there in your place? Of course not! So, the same is true for social media!

Remember, Facebook is truly about the long game. It's about the marathon and not the sprint. What you do today affects your business 6 months from now...12 months from now...18 months from now. Yes, there's a whole business strategy with pages and advertising and content. But the other side of that strategy is all of these little things that we do, day in and day out. It's the little things that will make a big difference.

Chapter 15

●　●　●

How to Optimize Your Facebook Personal Profile

In 2016, according to Pew Research, Facebook continues to be America's most popular social networking platform by a substantial margin: Nearly eight-in-ten *online* Americans (79%) now use Facebook. (http://www.pewinternet.org/2016/11/11/social-media-update-2016/)

And while the power of Facebook is growing, there is something more important to consider... the context of Facebook.

In addition to our connections, it's how we consume content on Facebook that is interesting to note. For example, 78% of Facebook users access Facebook on a mobile device. This is a huge statistic.

And if you think about your own experience using Facebook, you probably use it the same way most people do where you're out and about and then consume it kind of "in-between" your day. You're standing in line at the grocery, waiting to get a cup of coffee at Starbucks, in the car waiting to pick up your kids at school, and just sort of in-between moments. And if you're like me, you're holding your phone and your scrolling.

When you're on Facebook, you're competing with someone's best friend. You're competing with their husband, their wife, their kids, and more. It's a very personal environment.

Because of this, one of the things I always stress is that you are your brand. Many professionals come up to me and say, "Well, Katie, I've got my personal life over here, and I've got my professional life over here. And I really want to keep them separate." And as much as I respect and understand this, we're living in a world where it's not really black or white.

There's a lot of gray so let me talk about the personal profile, because this is a really key piece of your Facebook marketing. Like I said, people connect with you when you share who you are... beyond your business.

Getting intentional Using Facebook lists

If you haven't taken your Facebook friends and put them into some sort of organizational list, I can't emphasize enough how important this is. Now, I want to say, don't organize every single one of your friends on the list. That would take an enormous amount of time.

But there are a couple of lists I really recommend that you make.

Now, what's great about this is these lists are private so your clients aren't going to know they're on a list or the name of the list. And I recommend that you create two lists. One being a Client list (or you may call this a Customer list), which are people you're currently working with right now, maybe five, ten, fifteen people.

Quick tip: When you start working with someone, ask, "Are you on Facebook? I'd love to connect with you on Facebook." Then, you'll get a sense of whether or not they are a Facebook person. If not, make a note of it and know that they may be very private individuals. If they are on Facebook, connect with them and add them to your client list.

The second list you want to create is a Potential Client list. These are people that you might work with in the next 12 to 18 months. These are the people who say, "You know what? Contact me in six months and let's reconnect then." Your Potential Client list is going to be a lot larger with 20 to 30 people.

With your two lists, instead of looking at all of your Facebook friends, now you're going to see your list of ten clients. You'll see where they went to dinner last night, that their husband just got a job promotion, that they're going to apply in a couple of weeks, that their kids are going to start Little League in the spring, and more. And then, you just take five minutes to scroll through the posts and like, comment or share something on their posts.

Now, don't click or like everything because that's creepy. But take a few minutes to engage with people. Then, do the same thing with your Potential Client list. Click on potential clients, scroll through, see what people are talking about and engage with those people.

This is a really, really important thing. The reason why this is so important is because relationships are built with these small interactions over the course of time.

Every like, comment and share adds up. It's just like real life when you connect with someone at an event, then see them at the grocery store or somewhere, and then you connect with them on social media. Over time, you build a relationship with this person.

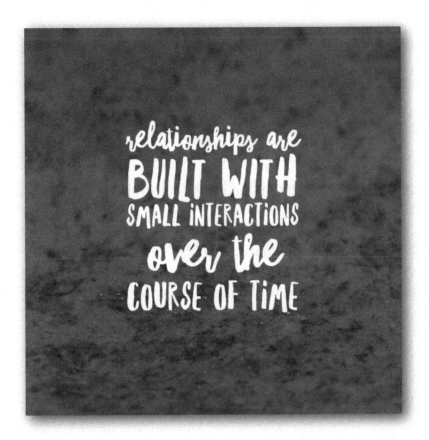

It's the same thing on Facebook. The beauty of this is it happens much faster. And for those people who say, "Contact me in six months," or "Contact me in 12 months," now you can stay top-of-mind with that person. They probably get put into a database for an email system, direct marketing, or other marketing processes too, but Facebook is a great way to keep in touch with these contacts in a really personal life. You connect with them on Facebook and then interact on things that are important to them. It's a little thing that makes a big difference.

Now, lists can only be made with personal profiles and your Facebook friends. This means that you're interacting with another person as yourself. It's just like when you go to a dinner party and you're talking to someone as you… not your business. This is the personal piece of Facebook and a really important concept. That's why allowing some of your clients, and some of your potential clients, to be a part of your personal Facebook life is important.

And once you create your lists, what can you post to help with these person-to-person communications?

Ideas for posts on your personal Facebook profile

Idea #1: Recognize one person publicly.

What if once a week or once a month, you went on your Facebook personal profile and you just recognized someone and gave them a shout-out? This, again, goes back to being intentional.

I intentionally try to do this at least once or twice a month and just say, "Hey, I just want to give a shout out to xyz. I want to give a shout out to my clients who are doing some amazing work, doing this blah, blah, blah, blah, blah."

When you recognize other people publicly in a form like Facebook, at the risk of sounding corny, it's a pretty magical thing.

Idea #2: Recognize a group or an organization that you're a part of publicly.

If you're a part of Rotary International, the local chamber of commerce, a political organization, or something else, recognize that group. Perhaps, you post something like, "Hey, I'm so excited to be a part of xyz because of this and this."

If you know your clients are part of an important organization, why not give your client a shout out along with that organization? And what I'm talking about here is really thinking thoughtfully about what you're putting up on Facebook. Sometimes, Facebook is a little bit of stream-of-conscious, or you just see people talking about the first thing that's on their mind. But, I want to challenge you to really think intentionally about who you can publicly recognize, and who you can publicly empower.

Idea #3: Share why you love what you do.

Obviously, you don't want to come across as bragging, but talk about your business in a way that shows why you love what you do. People want to work with those kind of people. That's how you stay top-of-mind to your friends and your family, versus the flip side which is venting. We all have tough days where we vent about our business. But think about who's watching that. You can vent personally to your friends, but share publicly why you love what you do.

Idea #4: Share something off-beat, funny or personal.

Again, this goes back to being personal on Facebook. Share something that only you can share that's personal, funny, off-beat and more.

Now, you may be wondering...

Do you need a personal Facebook Page and a business Profile?

My clients often ask me whether they really need two Facebook profiles, one personal and one business.

My answer: It depends on your own personal situation and your needs.

Your personal profile is a key part of your social-media strategy. This is where you're going to have information about yourself such as your family, hobbies, interests, and maybe a little about your business too. Your personal profile shouldn't be all about your business. In fact, that's against Facebook's Terms of Service.

That said, your personal profile is an important piece of how you connect with current and prospective clients. You might think, "Who cares about what I had for breakfast or about my dog photos?" Well, that's how you connect with people. You connect when people share things like photos of their kids, pets or even a great glass of wine that they had. And people want to do business with people they connect with.

At the heart of business are relationships. We do business with people we know, like and trust – and by connecting on your personal Facebook profile with clients and/or prospects is a great way to develop that relationship online.

You can also use your personal profile a little bit for business. I believe in the 80-20 rule: 80 percent personal, 20 percent business.

What should you talk about on your personal profile when it comes to business?

One of the most important things you can do is to celebrate moments. For example, think of the big things that happen in real estate, especially when you're working with a buyer or seller. It's such an emotional process, and sometimes we forget that. But you can document these moments (for example, when your clients are signing the paperwork, holding up the set of keys, standing by the sold sign, etc.). It's such a validating time for your clients.

Why not put that on your Facebook page with a photo or quick video to share how important this moment is to you and how you love what you do?

Quick tip: don't do this with your Facebook personal profile

What is one of the number one mistakes I see busy professionals make when they set up their Facebook personal profile?

They include other words into their name!

Too often I see a personal profile that says something like "Jane Smith, Realtor," instead of just, "Jane Smith."

Facebook's Terms of Service prohibits using anything but your name on your personal profile. This includes titles. The Terms of Service also explicitly forbid using a personal profile primarily for business. That's what business pages are for!

Now, this doesn't mean you can't incorporate your business into your personal profile. You just have to do it in a smart way. For example, you can share exciting moments such as when a first-time homebuyer closes on her new property, or the moment you hand over the keys to a new home.

I always say, "share why you love what you do." When you come from a place of loving what you do and are passionate about what you do, it is in the right context when it appears on your Facebook personal profile. Since these moments are a major reason you love being a real-estate agent, they're perfectly appropriate to share on your personal profile alongside your other interests!

Setting up the Follow feature on your Facebook personal profile

Sure, your friends enjoy seeing your posts on Facebook. However, you may be surprised to learn that it's not only your friends who are taking an interest in your experiences and thoughts. There are others out there who may want to know more about what you post and would like to have access to it. In addition, there may be some information you'd like to post publicly to help grow your business and connect with people you are not friends with yet on Facebook.

That's where the Facebook Follow feature (https://www.facebook.com/about/follow) comes in. If you decide that you would like people other than just your friends to know what's going on in your world, you can edit your settings to let yourself be followed. It's simple!

Adding the follower-option is an easy way to expand your online presence and get the word out about who you are and what you do.

Think about it this way. When you have followers, it's your audience coming to you! Followers give you a wider marketing-audience, more fans and greater credibility. You simply can't turn that down.

What do you do about Friend requests you aren't sure about?

We've all had that awkward moment. The moment we receive a friend request from someone we aren't sure if we want to friend or not. It could be that person you just met at a get-together, the friend-of-a-friend, your co-worker, and others. Do you say "yes" or "no"?

Well, the response is a personal choice. But when you have the follower feature enabled on your profile, even if you don't accept the request, that person will automatically follow you. Of course, if you would rather they not follow you, you can always deny the request.

What if you've reached the maximum number of friends?

If you have reached the maximum number of friends allowed on Facebook (5,000), adding followers is a great way to connect with more people.

Choose to post to Public or to Friends.

Facebook has nuanced its settings so that when you post, you can choose whether your audience isPublic or Friends. A good rule of thumb is to keep posts public if you're talking about your business. But you might choose to just post personal things to your friends. This is a good time to review your privacy settings, and you can adjust the audience you are posting to from your desktop or mobile-device too.

And here are a few other things that you may not know you can do with your personal profile!

Organize your favorites or shortcuts to find your most frequently visited places on Facebook

This is an amazing tool that allows you to add lists, groups or pages to your left side bar in Facebook as well as make things easily accessible from your smartphone. By default, Facebook will add items to your favorites for you, but there's a huge opportunity here that many miss. Take a few minutes to organize your favorites by what is most important to you. This will place your most important Facebook-activity front and center when accessing by desktop or mobile device. Some of my Favorites include:

- Client list
- Potential client list
- Past clients
- My Facebook Business Page
- My top interest lists
- My Facebook groups I manage

Facebook Messenger - connect one-to-one

Facebook Messenger is a great app for individuals and businesses to respond one-to-one to business inquiries or to connect with people one-to-one on

Facebook. I truly believe one of the most underutilized strategy within social media is the power of the one-to-one.

For example, the next time you have a killer piece of content you've created like a Facebook Live broadcast, blog post, video or podcast – before you blast it out on your social channels, think about the two or three people you could tell about it first. Who can you reach out to and say, *"Hi___! Just wanted to give you a heads up – we just published this and I wanted to send this to you first because_____. Would love your feedback on it. Feel free to share it out too here on FB. Thank you!"*

What a lot of people don't know is that you can actually leave voice messages using Facebook Messenger. To access this feature you need to download the Facebook Messenger app.

Within the app, you'll see a little microphone-icon. By pushing it, you can leave up to a one-minute audio message. This is a fantastic tool for connecting with people as there's just something special about hearing someone's voice. I especially love this for birthdays. Instead of being one of the hundreds of people to leave a Happy Birthday message on someone's wall, try leaving them a voice message instead. What a fun way to surprise and delight people!

Now let's talk more about Twitter....

Chapter 16

●　　●　　●

Twitter Tips and Strategies: #NoTweetLeftBehind

I t's time to tweet! While everyone approaches the Twitterverse differently, there are a few, important steps that, when taken, will make your overall experience far richer.

Check out these 10 steps to get set up the right way on Twitter:

1. **Pick a short, but memorable, username.**

   Your own name is best. Keep in mind that this is the way that you'll be identified throughout Twitter so it should be representative of how you'd like to be known on the site.

2. **Choose a strong profile-image.**

   It's important that you do this before you start to tweet. If you're tweeting on behalf of your business, using your company logo will act as a familiar association for your customers. If this is a personal account, use a clear headshot.

3. **Complete a bio with a link to your site.**

    Keep in mind that you only have 160 characters to explain who you are and what you do so give this a little thought before leaping into the task.

4. **Now that you've set up the basics of your Twitter account, it's time to send your first tweet.**

    This serves as an introduction to the Twitter community, so make it simple and cordial, as well as reflective of the personality you want to project!

5. **Connect with people you know.**

    Chances are that you already know people on Twitter. Adding them is a simple way to grow your network. It's also a chance to get to know them in a whole, new realm and perhaps, learn things about them that you didn't know previously.

6. **Connect with people local to you.**

    Using the Twitter search-function, you can find users in your local area, including other, local businesses that may be good to follow and get to know. If you're using Twitter for business, it's helpful to get a sense of how other, local businesses in your realm are doing it.

7. **Let your network know you're on Twitter.**

    If you send a tweet and no one reads it, what's the point? Put the word out to your network on your email list, company newsletter and your other, social networks.

8. **Join the conversation.**

    Jump into Twitter chats using @Twubs or @TweetChat. Remember, one of the biggest benefits to Twitter is the two-way conversation that can happen!

9. **Select a Twitter client that lets you manage multiple accounts.**

    HootSuite and SproutSocial are both great options and will allow you to schedule your tweet and monitor key conversations.

10. **Tweet, tweet, tweet.**

    Whether you're sharing blog posts, photos and videos, or simply helpful observations and information, make use of this medium. Don't forget to have fun!

Twitter basics explained

What's with the @ sign?

Everyone's handle is preceded by the "at" (@) sign. If you start a tweet with someone's handle, the only people who see that tweet are those who follow both you and them. If you include the handle in the middle of your tweet, it's open to the public.

DM: A private Twitter message is known as a Direct Message, or DM.

The re-tweet: By re-tweeting, you're taking an existing tweet and sharing it with your followers.

Must-dos to rock your Twitter strategy:

1. **Tweet with images in order to increase engagement.**
   Tweets with images receive more click-throughs, more favorites and more re-tweets.
2. **Repeat tweets.**
   You can repeat any type of content that you've created, including blog posts and videos. Remember, Twitter moves fast so tweeting the same content over the course of days/weeks is a great way to drive traffic back to your site. Make sure to mix up these tweets with other content.
3. **Tweet links to other articles with some commentary.**
   Link clicks account for an astounding 92 percent of all user-interaction with tweets. I love to tweet interesting articles, making sure to tag the source in the tweet.
4. **Create lists (twitter.com/lists.) to get intentional and organized with whom you want to connect.**
   Ideas for lists include: Clients, News, Authors, Photographers, College Friends, etc.

5. **Use lists to curate content.**

Lists are a great way to curate content or look for relevant content for your business. For example, if you are a real-estate professional, you may create a list of local, business owners as a way to connect with them and curate great, local content.

6. **Find local content.**

Search your market area and follow key media-outlets. Use http://search.twitter.com to search specific cities and keywords.

7. **Be a good finder!**

Look for opportunities to highlight people doing good things in your community and re-tweet them! Show what it feels like to live in your community by re-tweeting local groups and news channels, showcasing photos and putting text over your photos.

Here are the things to avoid and the top five ways that you can fail at Twitter (don't take this as a to-do list!):

- Spamming people over and over again with your promotion, sale, real-estate listing, etc.
- Constant self-promotion. It's less about you and more about the value you can bring the people who follow you.
- Auto-messages. If you have an auto-DM every time someone follows you, turn that off. It's very spam-like!
- Not responding to messages. Make sure when people tweet you or mention you that you respond with either a quick tweet back or even just "liking" the tweeting. #NoTweetLeftBehind! This is especially important if you are scheduling some tweets. Make sure you go back and respond and engage!
- Connecting your Facebook to Twitter. When you connect your Facebook to Twitter, some of the message gets lost on Twitter. If all you are doing is pushing content from Facebook to Twitter, you are sending the message that "the lights are on, but no one is really home."

What the heck is a hashtag?

A hashtag is either a searchable term like #realestate, #fashion, or it's something that's said a bit "tongue-in-cheek" like #justsayin.

Hashtags are a way to filter through the noise.

Twitter can be like a cocktail party with people at one table talking about their kids, another table talking about vacation plans, another talking about the holidays and another talking business. And, at any point, you can go up to one particular table and join the conversation. With hashtags, you can locate those conversations and join them more easily.

Additionally, using Twitter's Advanced Search (http://search.twitter.com) feature, you can search hashtags based on geography. This can be particularly helpful for people who are #househunting.

There's also a fun, cheeky side to hashtags. These are hashtags that don't necessarily have a purpose, but are more of a fun way of saying something, like, #youknowwhatimean?

I hope that helps clear up the issue a bit!

Now, let's get into photos and Twitter…

5 creative ways to use photos on Twitter

Photos on Twitter are becoming more important than ever before. Looking to take your Twitter strategy to the next level and increase re-tweets and favorites?

Check out my 5 creative ways to use photos on Twitter:

1. Add a filter.
2. Tag friends.
3. Crop photos.
4. Upload multiple images.
5. Send photos privately.

Photos can add more to your Twitter posts to help engage current followers, and bring in new ones.

And here's another tip…

Have you checked out your free Twitter analytics?

Ever wonder who exactly is following you on Twitter, how engaging your tweets are or how many people are clicking on the links you tweet them?

Check out free, Twitter analytics!

If you love a good "hack" like me, you'll love this.

- Go to http://ads.twitter.com.
- Log in with your Twitter credentials.
- Click Analytics at the top and then choose what analytics you want to see.

Best part? This is a free service from Twitter!

This type of content can help you decide which content resonates the most with your audience, which links were most effective and so much more.

Now, let's move on to some LinkedIn insights…

* * *

Chapter 17

How to Maximize LinkedIn

LinkedIn is a great place to start because it's the largest, professional social-media-network. Unfortunately, it often becomes a set-it-and-forget-it network, meaning you set it up and haven't done much with it since.

It's important to keep your LinkedIn profile updated. After all, when potential clients search for you on Google or Bing, one of the top sites that will appear is LinkedIn. If your profile is outdated, it gives the perception that you are out of business.

Here are a few, simple tips to maximize your LinkedIn profile.

Step 1: Update your profile

Background

- Include name, title and company

Summary

- Update your summary. This should be two to three paragraphs that are an overview of your experience and expertise.

Upload presentations

- If you have presentations formatted in Key Note or Power Point about a particular topic, you can upload these in the section below your expertise. You can also connect your SlideShare account to LinkedIn and add presenstations to your profile.

Experience

- Make sure you have the basics in there including an updated photo, work history (last 10 years), dates, experience, and education.

Skills and expertise

- Think of this section as the "keywords" for your profile. Pick seven to ten keywords that describe your specialties and/or areas of expertise.

People can endorse you for these skills, and you can also suggest additional skills that may not be listed.

Step 2: Recommendations

One of the biggest benefits of LinkedIn are the recommendations you can receive. To the average consumer, LinkedIn testimonials are more authentic because you did not touch or alter them in any way. They are truly from a past colleague or client. This is "social proof."

Write one or two recommendations a month for: fellow co-workers, agents, title reps, mortgage lenders, and/or your stager(s), and other business associates. A recommendation is unexpected, but it is almost always appreciated and reciprocated.

A recommendation can be two or three sentences of how you know this person and why you would recommend them.

Step 3: Driving traffic to your LinkedIn profile

Add your public-profile link to your email signature. If you are using Outlook, edit your email signature in the Edit>Options menu. If you are using Gmail or another free, email provider, a great free service to use is WiseStamp. WiseStamp will allow you to add all your social media channels into your email signature.

Include connections; Add past and current colleagues and clients. It's worth the time to get your client database into an excel spreadsheet (.CSV file) and add it to LinkedIn.

Also, be sure to add every, new person you meet that could be a potential client. It's easier to send a LinkedIn request than a Facebook Friend request to someone you just met!

Step 4: LinkedIn status updates

Get in front of your connections on LinkedIn by posting a status update to LinkedIn three times a week.

Do's:

- Post links to articles about the market (from industry sites, Inman News, Realtor Magazine, local associations, brokerage/franchise, and more.)
- It is recommended that most of your posts on LinkedIn are professional and focus on things like your business activities, industry news, related-events, and more.

Don'ts:

- Post links to listings or personal updates (i.e. family or hobbies).
- Include so many posts that it's annoying and creates a bad impression of your business. Whatever you post, remember to keep your brand image in mind.

Step 5: Publishing content to LinkedIn

By publishing once or twice a month on LinkedIn, it continues to establish your credibility throughout your professional network. There is tremendous value in publishing new or old blog posts on the LinkedIn platform. If your post gains a lot of traction, it can be viewed by thousands of people beyond your connections!

Do's

- Post original content. Get creative and provide interesting information.
- Include a photo in your post. Create a free image using Canva.com.

- At the end of your post, add two to three sentences about who you are, and link back to your original post (if this was a post you previously wrote).

Don'ts

- Copy/paste articles from other sources or articles that you did not originally write. Note: You can see examples of all of these items at http://linkedin.com/in/katielance

Great! Your LinkedIn account is up and running. How do you monitor the results?

If you are creating a Company or Showcase Page on LinkedIn, it's not enough to assume that you're getting a decent number of visitors. That's where LinkedIn's powerful Analytics come in. They offer an at-a-glance idea of how your pages are performing and who you may not be reaching. In addition, you can see how individual posts are performing along with the engagement rate of key metrics.

Well, what if you looked at your analytics and didn't like your numbers? What can you do to improve them?

10 ways to optimize your LinkedIn blog posts

There is a lot of value to publishing blog posts on LinkedIn. Personally, I've seen many benefits to publishing new content and also re-purposing older ("evergreen") content on LinkedIn.

I found that since LinkedIn is a much quieter network, I am able to get in front of more of my connections (and their connections) by providing valuable insight. I've seen it help to increase my followers on LinkedIn, traffic back to my site, and ultimately, leads that have led to business.

Recently, a study by OkDork (http://okdork.com/) and Search Wilderness (http://searchwilderness.com/) was released that studied 3,000 of the highest performing pieces of content on LinkedIn and what made them so successful.

Here are their findings:

1. **Optimal title length:** It's 40-49 characters.
2. **Title format:** Titles should not be questions. These tend to perform worse than titles that are short statements.
3. **Images:** Eight images are best and perform almost three times better than those with less!
4. **Video is not as effective:** Unlike other, social-media platforms, video posts perform significantly lower than posts without video.
5. **Subheadings:** Posts with exactly five subheadings performed best.
6. **Word count:** 1,900-2000 words is ideal.
7. **Neutral sentiment:** Posts on LinkedIn that were neutral performed 70% better.
8. **Easy to read:** Make it so easy that a middle-schooler can read it!
9. **Likes:** Once your post is "liked," it is viewable to more, second-tier connections.
10. **Day of the week:** Thursday is the best day for publishing!

At this point, you may have amassed hundreds, or even thousands, of LinkedIn connections. It can be overwhelming and chaotic. So here are…

3 easy tips to maximize LinkedIn

You now have an organized, LinkedIn profile. And for any professional, this can be a huge opportunity to connect with your current sphere as well as deepen professional relationships with people you recently met.

How else can you maximize LinkedIn?

Here are my three, favorite tips:

1. **LinkedIn is where social starts.**

   Connect on LinkedIn with every new person you meet that can be a client. Reach out to potential and current clients via LinkedIn. This is an easy way to connect and expand your sphere professionally. It's where to start in social. After all, it's easier to send a LinkedIn request than a Facebook Friend request to someone you just met! Make sure you send a personal note with your request, something like: "Hi (name), it was great to meet you at (event). I'd love to connect with you on LinkedIn. –(yourname)."

2. **Post a status update daily 3-5 times a week.**

   LinkedIn Today is a great source of content and includes articles written by thought leaders on LinkedIn. Stay active on LinkedIn. Post articles about your industry, and stay top of mind for the professionals who come across your profile. If the last time you posted something was last year, it can give the perception that you are "out of business."

3. **Give to get.**

   Give one new recommendation a month to someone you have worked with recently. Who can you thank for their business and service this month? A colleague? A client? Look at who you are interacting with, and make an intentional point to say thank you publicly. One of the best ways to do this is through a LinkedIn recommendation.

You've got this. Now, onto Snapchat…

Chapter 18

◉ ◉ ◉

Snapchat for Business

re you on Snapchat yet? With 100M users and 400M snaps a day, Snapchat is quickly becoming a major player in the social-media world (source: http://expandedramblings.com/index.php/snapchat-statistics/)

Here are some other staggering statistics about Snapchat:

- 30% of U.S. Millennial Internet users access Snapchat regularly
- 65% of Snapchat daily users contribute content
- 18% of all US social media users use Snapchat

(source: http://expandedramblings.com/index.php/snapchat-statistics/)

Snapchat is a very real platform, meaning it's in the moment and authentic. As a social-media strategist, I believe this is where the future of social media is going. I think people are tired of only seeing the best version of ourselves - the filtered Instagram photos or the highlights of our life on Facebook. It's not that Facebook and Instagram don't have an important place in your social-media strategy. I just see a different type of authenticity with Snapchat. With apps like <u>Periscope</u> and Snapchat, we are getting more raw interactions, something I think people are craving.

I was hesitant about Snapchat at first because the content disappears after 24 hours. I didn't understand the point of spending time to create content that was just going to disappear. But, now that I'm on the platform, I realize that Snapchat is not about creating beautiful pieces of content that are going to last forever and ever. Rather, it's about capturing small snippets throughout your day that help to tell the story of who you are. I'm a big believer in the power of using social media to craft your story and showing people what it's like to work with you. This is why I now believe that Snapchat is an amazing platform, and I encourage you to integrate it into your social strategy.

Snapchat Basics: Getting Started

Your profile.

Let's take a look at your Snapchat profile. Unique to Snapchat, your profile photo is a series of four photos which create a moving image. You'll also find your Snapcode on your profile. This is one of the easiest ways for people to find and connect with each other on the platform and why you may see screenshots of Snapcodes being shared on other social networks.

Connecting with other Snapchatters.

You can search by username or by Snapcode. If you see someone's Snapcode online (like on Twitter or Facebook), you will want to save that Snapcode to your Camera Roll in your phone. Then, when you go to Snapchat, click "Add Friends," "Add by Snapcode." You will see your Camera Roll, and you can easily add someone as a friend by clicking on their Snapcode.

Your followers.

Another unique thing about Snapchat is that it's not really about how many friends or followers you have. In fact, if you click through to your friends-list you'll notice they don't give you a number. They do offer a feature called "Best Friends," which are people you interact with frequently.

Snap basics.

Ok. Now it's time to snap! Snaps can be photos or videos up to 15 seconds. When you go to Snap, you are basically doing one of two things: sending a snap to one person or sending a snap to "Your Story." Your Story is something you can contribute to and it will share your snaps for the past 24 hours. Most of the time, this is how I am using Snapchat.

Your Snapchat story.

Your Story is a great way to showcase a behind-the-scenes look at your life and business. Check out my story on Snapchat (https://www.snapchat.com/add/katielance1) to see how I've been using it. One very powerful feature of your story is the ability to see who has viewed your content. To do this, click on your story, and then click the eye icon to view the list.

Here are a few features to know about creating your snaps:

- Add text, drawings or an emoji to your snap. Have fun – draw and doodle over your snaps!
- Add additional features like the date, time and other geo-filters
- Create your own custom geo-filters by going to Snapchat.com and following the instructions for personal or business use.

You've created your profile, connected with some friends and started snapping. Now what?

What to Snap?

Think about what type of content you want to share on Snapchat. You may want to share a "behind-the-scenes" sneak peek into your day, quick tips and lessons-learned, promote your other channels (i.e. a new blog post or Periscope), funny or silly moments, and more. I love Snapchat for sharing the 'story behind the story.' For example, I may share one or two photos from an event on Facebook or Instagram, but on Snapchat tells the story on the way to the event, during and even after!

An important reminder: If you use Snapchat for business, please avoid using 100% of your content to talk about business. It's just like any other social-media-platform – No one wants to tune into you if the only thing you talk about is your blog, your product, your service, your website, etc.!

How can business owners leverage Snapchat?

Here are a few ideas and resources for making the most of it for business.

Give a sneak-peek behind the scenes. For my business, I've used Snapchat to share fun travel stories as I crisscross the country for speaking engagements; I also love to share quick tips and 'the story behind the story' of what you may see on Facebook or Instagram. Are you a Realtor? You can showcase a sneak-peek into your day; working with clients, the process of your day, highlights from the neighborhoods you visit, and just how hard you work for your clients!

Promoting live events. Are there live events you are at in your local community you could Snap and share? If you are nervous about being on-camera, this is a great place to start!

Have fun with the platform. Get a little silly and creative, and don't be afraid to show a more personal side of you! Think in terms of stories and what story can you tell each day about your business? If you already have a strategy in place for other platforms – can that be cross-pollinated on Snapchat too? For example, you may post a #MondayMotivation graphic every Monday on Instagram. Using that theme – could you share 5-10 motivational quotes on Snapchat on Monday? Consistency and repurposing content is key!

Create custom geo-filters. You can now easily create a custom geo-filter for your business by going to https://www.snapchat.com/on-demand. This is a great way to increase exposure for anyone using Snapchat in the location of your business. Imagine doing this for an Open House, a local concert or any local gathering. The potential brand exposure is exciting.

Partner with influencers. We are seeing brands and influences do a "Snap Swap" where they will swap accounts for the day, or businesses will have influencers take over their account for a day. Social media influencers can help spread brand awareness and reach. By partnering with key Snapchat influencers in your area, you can spread awareness to a demographic that's hard to reach through traditional media. Are there other Snappers in your area? Swap accounts for a day to grow your Snapchat presence.

Advertise. Depending on your budget, there are some exciting options for advertising on Snapchat. According to Snapchat, here is the breakdown on Snapchat advertising options (all of these stats can be found at Snapchat. com):

- **Snap ads.** Snap Ads offer the best in mobile video ads with the choice to add an interactive element below. Snap Ads always begin with an up to 10-second vertical, full screen video ad that appears in the context of other Snaps. You can also give Snapchatters the choice to swipe up and see more, just like they do elsewhere on Snapchat. Swiping up reveals extended content like a long form video, article, app install ad, or mobile website. The swipe-up rate for Snap Ads is **5x higher** than the average click-through rate on comparable platforms.
- **Sponsored Geofilters.** Sponsored Geofilters are tiny pieces of art that always make an impression. When Snapchatters in the location(s) of your choice take a Snap, they'll be able to see your Geofilter and use it to explain where, when, and why they took the Snap. Whether your campaign covers a specific location, a major event, or every mall in America, Geofilters uniquely allow brands to take part in the hundreds of millions of Snaps sent between friends each day on Snapchat. In the US, a single National Sponsored Geofilter typically reaches **40% to 60%** of daily Snapchatters.
- **Sponsored Lenses.** Sponsored Lenses offer a completely new take on brand activation, offering not just an impression, but "play time" — the time Snapchatters spend playing with the interactive ad you've

created. To activate Lenses, Snapchatters simply press and hold on their faces. Some Lenses include prompts like "raise your eyebrows" to trigger an animation, adding a fun twist to the experience. And when you're finished playing, it's easy to send Lenses to a friend or post one to your Story. On average, Snapchatters play with a Sponsored Lens for **20 seconds**.

Have fun!

While you may be using Snapchat for business, don't forget to have fun! This social-media platform provides the perfect opportunity to get a little silly and creative. Don't be afraid to show a more personal side of you!Now, let's talk about live video, Periscope, Facebook Live, and more...

Chapter 19

● ● ●

Live Video, Periscope, Facebook Live and More!

The buzz in the air is palpable. live video (or live streaming) is taking the so-cial-media world by storm. In just a few short months, Periscope, the live-streaming video app from the creators of Twitter, has amassed over 10 million users (me being a very enthusiastic one of them!) In fact, I can't remember being this excited about a new social platform for a very, very long time.

So why am I so excited about Periscope and Facebook Live, and for that matter, live streaming in general? Well, for starters, it gives anyone and ev-eryone the ability to live-stream content right from their iPhone or Android device. In addition to live streaming, Periscope and Facebook Live allows users to watch broadcasters live and in real time, communicating through comments and hearts (or likes.)

Why is live video so significant?

As I wrote in The Huffington Post (http://www.huffingtonpost.com/au-thor/katie-lance), I believe that live video is set to transform the number of companies and individuals who are focusing on social media. That's due to Periscope and Facebook Live's unique ability to broadcast anywhere in the world. With literally the push of a button, you're communicating with anyone who wishes to tune in.

This is incredible in a society that sees so many of us living in our own little bubble with our family, professions, daily to-do task-lists, and more. So often, we believe that we have barely enough time to see what is going on in the world around us.

However, live video has opened my eyes and clarified my vision. The first week that I used Periscope, I experienced the most vivid dreams. But, I think a large part of that was the opportunity to view the world not simply through a filtered television show, but through the eyes of a real person with experiences and insights to share. For the first time, people like you and me thought, "This is worth sharing – live!"

I'm extremely grateful for that brand of generosity. Because of it, I've met some incredibly talented musicians, comedians, inspirational coaches, health and wellness experts, artists, scientists, tech and marketing leaders, and so many others.

As for broadcasting myself, when I first jumped on Periscope, I thought I would broadcast once a week. Now, I find myself broadcasting daily, sometimes several times a day, and have done over 500 broadcasts - and counting!

Why am I investing my time and energy into this platform?

Well, for one thing, there is an incredible community out there. When you work and consult in social media, you sometimes feel as though you exist in an echo chamber where you see and hear from the same people. Periscope gives me the chance to meet people from all walks of life – different ages, backgrounds and geographic locations – and it's so much fun!

But beyond that, I also see exponential potential for this exciting, new platform. It's already made a huge impact on my business, and I am confident, this is only the beginning. Like I always say, a successful, social-media-marketing strategy should be approached like a marathon, not a sprint. When it comes to Periscope, we've only just left the starting line, and I, for one, could not be more excited about what's to come!

How to start on Periscope

First, you need to download the Periscope app. If you've got a Twitter account, you can create your account there. And, even if you're not a Twitter user, you can still create a Periscope account.

To start engaging with the Periscope community, find existing and new friends, and start watching broadcasts. If you like what you see, follow the broadcaster. You can communicate with broadcasters by leaving comments or hearts (the latter is a great way to offer validation to them and create a relationship).

Pro tip: Use emojis in your bio to make it pop!

Connect with friends and followers.

If you already have a Twitter account, you can connect with any of your Twitter friends who are on Periscope with the click-of-a-button.

Pro tip: One of the best ways to make new connections on Periscope is to watch a variety of broadcasts. Read the titles, and join broadcasts that you think may interest you. Comment and engage with the broadcaster. If you enjoy the content, share the broadcast with your followers too. One of the fastest ways to grow your own following is to be engaged in the community.

How to start with Facebook Live

Facebook Live is available to anyone who has the Facebook app on their phone (or the Facebook Pages app for business pages.) You simply go to the screen where you would normally post a status update or post a photo, and there will be an icon to "go live!" Once you push that button, you will receive a prompt from Facebook reminding you that you are going live. Then, you will see a countdown of when you will go live.

Once you broadcast live on Facebook, anyone can watch, like or comment via a mobile device or computer. And when you are ready to end the broadcast, your live video will stay on your page.

Pro tip: Once you go live, say "Hi" to everyone, let them know what you are going to talk about and then, wait a few seconds for people to start watching or commenting. If you don't get a high amount of interaction right away, don't get discouraged. Many times, people comment later once they see the video recording in their feed. In fact, I have found that I get more viewers on my replays than my live video!

What do I need to know about broadcasting?

Here are my top 10 broadcasting tips:

1. **Prepare with a plan.** Know what you want to share but stay flexible in order to field audience comments and questions. I suggest writing down three to five bullet points in advance. You also want to think about the headline of your broadcast. I recommend that it be catchy, short and have a unique hashtag or two.

2. **Toggle the camera.** Double tap the screen to switch the camera between you and your audience. Keep in mind that there is a sound delay while doing this so pause while you're speaking.

3. **Decide whether or not to enable location** Users can now search broadcasts by map-location, but if you're not comfortable broadcasting from a private place (like your home), this may not work for you. That said, if you're running a location-based business such as a restaurant or retail store, this could be a great feature to drive local, foot traffic!

4. **Save your broadcasts.** While your broadcasts will auto-save to your phone, I also like to sync my videos to Dropbox (www.dropbox.com) so that they won't take up too much of my phone's memory.

5. **Do not disturb.** Before beginning a live broadcast, put your phone in Airplane mode or Do Not Disturb mode so that you won't be interrupted by calls.

6. **Say hello.** Kick off a broadcast by speaking immediately, welcoming your audience and then introducing yourself.

7. **Get others engaged.** Ask and answer questions to make your broadcast about more than just you!

8. **Are you getting trolled?** Block them! It's simple. Just tap their name and click "block." Don't worry. Every social-media platform has trolls, but they are few and far between.

9. **Remind people to follow you and share your broadcast.** Do this at the beginning, and make sure you give them a reason why!

10. **Remember the Boy Scout rule and be prepared.** Promote your broadcasts on other, social networks before you air. And, add them to your calendar along with other, social media and content plans.

8 things you must-do once you go live

1. Start right away.
2. Introduce yourself - who are you, what are you going to talk about.
3. Welcome people to the room.
4. Invite people to follow you and share the broadcast.
5. Block the trolls by tapping on their name.
6. Ask for people to share the broadcast at the beginning, middle and end.
7. Thank people at the end.
8. Give a call-to-action. Where can people find out more about you? (your website, phone number, etc.)

Pro tip: Use a unique hashtag to brand you and your live video-shows!

How can I promote my live video?

When it comes to promoting your live video, there are a few things to consider. First, let's take a look at pre-marketing. If you have built a network on another, social channel(s), whether that's Twitter, a Facebook business page or even your personal Facebook profile, you can leverage that network to help build your live-video audience.

I suggest promoting your live video show on Facebook, Twitter, LinkedIn, and Instagram the day of your broadcast and/or 10 minutes before you go live. My favorite way to do this is by creating a graphic with your scope's subject, day and time using an app like Canva (www.canva.com/) or PicMonkey (www.picmonkey.com/).

Perhaps you have an email list? It's a great idea to include your upcoming, live-video shows in your email newsletter or other email marketing.

The next important piece of post-marketing is to share your replay. I like to share my replay immediately following the broadcast and then again the following day. I will share on Twitter, Facebook, and, depending on the content, via Instagram and LinkedIn too. When sharing the next day, I suggest sharing once in the morning and then again one-hour before the broadcast expires (for Periscope).

Now, let's talk post-marketing. After your broadcast is over, there are a couple of different opportunities. The first thing I suggest is to watch your broadcast.

It's a great idea to watch your broadcast simply to evaluate your delivery, and see where you can improve. But, it also allows you to identify and connect with people who are very active in your broadcasts. You can then follow those people on Periscope and even take it a step further by finding them on

Twitter and sending them a public "thank you!" We also embed some of our Periscope content (using YouTube into our blog to repurpose our content and to generate new, blog content.

Pro tip: Let's not forget the opportunity to reach out to people one-to-one. As you start to connect with people on Periscope (or other, live-stream platforms), consider doing a broadcast promoting other Periscopers. In fact, that's one of the ways I've been able to grow my following so quickly. Don't just think about the content you can push out, but also consider doing broadcasts to promote others.

And, be sure to include the day and time that your broadcast expires to create a sense of urgency and encourage people to take action. I've found that by creating a quick image and including that with my posts, I get a greater response.

I also like to include the length of my Periscope (i.e. quick 5-minute scope) so people can determine whether they have time to watch, or not. And remember to always include your unique hashtag,

Be intentional about connecting with people beyond Periscope by creating a Twitter list with your Periscope connections:

1. Go to twitter.com/lists to create a list of Periscope connections.
2. View that list a few times a week.
3. Engage, re-tweet.
4. Be authentic.

Finally, when it comes to marketing your live videos, you want to see how you can integrate it into your current, marketing activities. For example, are you conducting email marketing? Do you have a Facebook business page? Are you active on Instagram...or YouTube?

Before you jump into your Periscope marketing-strategy, I encourage you to take a step back and look at what you're already doing. There is no need to reinvent the wheel. For example, I am a regular blogger and post a new article to my blog at least twice a week. So when it came to developing content for my Periscope account, it only made sense to repurpose my blog content and turn it into scopes. This has not only provided me with tons of content for Periscope, but it also allows me to revisit and highlight past blog-posts — a win-win!

What about a content plan?

Another, key element to a successful live streaming strategy is to create a content plan. If you've been following me, you know I'm a big advocate of planning. I am a firm believer that using some sort of content grid or editorial calendar is critical to your social-media success. We use a simple Google Calendar to keep everything organized and easy to access.

Tips for a successful live video content plan:

1. Brainstorm a list of topics.
2. Decide on how often you'd like to broadcast and what time of day.
3. Consistency wins.
4. Repurpose existing content (i.e. blog content).
5. Use Google Calendar or a Google spreadsheet.

Jump in and do it! While your first live-video may not be perfect, that doesn't matter. Get in there, and I guarantee you'll meet some truly incredible people.

What's the future for live video?

The brilliance of these apps is that they open up a forum for a live audience to interact during a broadcast. They can ask questions and engage as part of the conversation. In the past, we had apps such as UStream, which acted as a streaming video platform. But, never have so many people, from all walks of life, had the ability to take a photo or video and live-stream it.

Personally, I've already seen live video transform the way in which I consume news. I hear and see many stories before they appear on mainstream media. We've been seeing this on Facebook and Twitter for years, but the difference is that this isn't just a tweet or Facebook update in real time. Rather, it's someone streaming live for the world to see.

Who will see long-term success with live video?

Those who aren't simply broadcasting to receive accolades, but those willing to put in the work to build trust with other people in the community; this happens over time by providing great content, being authentic and not simply having your scopes focus on you as the broadcaster. It's the same formula that works when it comes to Facebook, Twitter or any other social-network.

This dovetails with what I always say… It's less about you and more about them.

Next on the horizon with live video is now Instagram Live and the same rules apply; have a strategy, be consistent and have fun with it!

Building and keeping trust online in the 21st century is one of our most precious commodities. This goes for Periscope and other, live-streaming apps as well. Think of trust as the ultimate game leveler; what's relevant is not whether you're the most privileged or popular, but rather how genuine and real you are. It doesn't get more real than pointing the camera at yourself and broadcasting live to the world, and I can't wait to see what comes next!

"Remember, like with any social media platform, it's less about you and more about them."

Chapter 20

●　●　●

How to Figure Out Which Social Media Platforms to Be On

There are a lot of social platforms to choose from: Facebook, Twitter, Snapchat, Instagram, Pinterest, YouTube, LinkedIn, and the list goes on and on.

I'd like to take a step back and look at why most people ask which platform they should be on. For most people, they ask this question because they are either:

1. Not on social media at all and wondering where to start, OR
2. Overwhelmed with social media (and sometimes feel like it's a big time suck!)

If you fall into either one of these buckets - you are like a lot of people! When it comes to where to start in social media, it really depends on two factors: which platforms you really love and which platforms your clients are using the most.

For example, in real estate, I generally recommend that if a real estate pro is going to start anywhere that they start on LinkedIn, and make sure their profile is up to date because when a potential client searches for you online - if they come upon an outdated or non-existent profile, there is the perception that you aren't in business.

I also generally recommend that a real estate pro spend some time on Facebook for two reasons; on their personal profile to connect and stay in touch with their clients and on their business Page to grow their sphere and their book of business.

Now, this advice is somewhat general and applies to many people in real estate, but for those of you reading this - you may not like Facebook, or you may be tired of all the noise on Facebook, or maybe your clients aren't there too. So, for you - Instagram may be a better place for you or even Snapchat. Or maybe you love how fast Twitter moves; it's quick, simple with 140 characters, and that's where you enjoy spending your time.

I was chatting with a broker recently who was telling me how for Facebook and Instagram - he is focused on creating polished content that adheres to his brand standard, but that Snapchat and Facebook Live were so freeing to him - that he absolutely loved the platform. In just a few short weeks his strategy has paid off - he's already been featured in various articles and online as an early adopter and one to watch in real estate when it comes to Snapchat and Facebook Live.

So, the question remains - where do you LIKE spending your time?

What I've found is that a lot of people blow off a platform because they don't think they understand it or think it's a waste of time - only to realize that if they would have given it a chance, it may be perfect for them. I also think a lot of people devalue where they like because they wonder if their clients are there. What I have found is that - when you are doing what you love (especially online) - your tribe will follow.

Periscope for me is a great example. When I first joined Periscope, there were maybe a handful of my friends and clients on there. But, I fell in love with the platform and started spending a ton of time there, getting to know the community and the results one year later - is that I am now known to be very active on Periscope, I have more and more of my clients there every day and the new tribe I have met and connected with - are people I may not have ever connected with if it weren't for Periscope!

So, here's your homework assignment this week. Yep, you are going to have homework!

- Block off an hour this week and spend some time in Facebook, Twitter, Instagram, Pinterest, Snapchat, Twitter, and Periscope.
- At a minimum, pick 3 and spend some time in each of them exploring the features, clicking around, searching for things that are of interest to you and decide which platforms you are going to invest more time in.

I think sometimes we worry that doing this is a waste or time - just 'surfing around.' But, how can you dismiss something if you haven't ever tried it? I sheepishly raise my hand to say that is how I felt about Snapchat. For the longest time, I felt like Snapchat wasn't for me and I hadn't even tried it. But, once I downloaded it and actually took the time to learn it - then I realized it was quickly becoming one of my favorite platforms!

Now, the second big question remains: where are your clients at online? Again, for a lot of us we assume - we assume our clients aren't on Snapchat or Twitter - because we aren't.

So, here is your second homework assignment (yep, there are two!)

- Write a list of your 10 current clients (either current clients you are working with now or your 10 most recent clients.) This list can be on a spreadsheet or just written down on a post-it.

- Then, I want to you to block off another hour. In this hour, I want you to Google each client, but what I want you to do is Google them with quotes around their name like this: "Katie Lance." Look to see what comes up on page 1 in Google. Now, if their name is common, you may need to search their name and city, such as "Katie Lance" + Their City.
- This list will give you a good start of where they are online. Look at the top 5-10 links - if they are Twitter, Facebook, LinkedIn or others, you are looking for two things: is their profile up-to-date (i.e. recent photo) but more importantly, when is the last time they posted? If the last time they posted was in 2012 (or they aren't on the platform at all, it's a pretty good assumption they are not on there at all.)
- Make a note on that spreadsheet or post-it of where they seem to be most active and a link to that account.
- If you are active on the platforms they are active on, connect with them there!
- Lastly, I want to you to send a personal email individually to each of these 10 people and say something like this (feel free to copy and paste and edit as needed):

Hi _____,

Hope all is well! I am doing an informal survey to see which of my clients are on Snapchat. Are you active there? Let me know either way - thank you!

Katie

The reason this email is so important is that Snapchat is one of the fastest growing social media platforms; however it can be really challenging to know if your clients are there or not because the way you discover people in Snapchat is different than any other platform.

Also, this simple email asks a simple question - if they are on Snapchat then great - you can connect with them there - but if they aren't, that's ok too and you may have a dialog back and forth about where they are or are not on social media.

So, the question remains - how are you going to figure out once and for all which platforms to be on? The answer is really simple; where do you like to be and where are your clients at? Once you have answered that - then you can move onto creating content and creating a strategy that will help you keep in touch more effectively with your clients and will build your brand and your business.

Just remember - success in social media is a marathon and not a sprint.

I don't expect to get a ton of business from Snapchat tomorrow - but I do see the rewards down the line, just like I have seen with other social platforms. If you are curious about how I personally use each platform and my 'secret sauce' for tying them together - you should read this post.

I'd love to hear from you once you read this and also once you complete your homework assignments. Send me a Tweet @katielance and use the hashtag #GetSocialSmart!

Chapter 21

●　　●　　●

Social-Media Tools and Resources

The world of social-media is constantly changing. I'll provide a few tools to help you below, but for the latest resources and updates, please visit my Website at www.katielance.com. Also, these are all products we personally use and believe in… you won't see anything listed below that hasn't been tried and tested!

Email marketing and management

Email is like the "kissing cousin to social media." Although this book isn't focused on email, having an integrated, email-marketing plan has had a significant part in taking social-media to the next level for us, and our clients.

- **Unroll.Me**

   Ready to take back control of your email and get one step closer to inbox zero? I love Unroll.me for helping to mass-unsubscribe, or just manage my email subscriptions.

- **Mailchimp.**

   Mailchimp is a great place to start with your email marketing. We have used Mailchimp for close to three years. With its simple interface and easy-to-use app, we loved it for building our email newsletter list.

In fact, our Saturday email newsletter is one of the things that people compliment me and our team on the most!

- **Infusionsoft.**

  We took the plunge and decided to move from Mailchimp to Infusion Soft. As our lists and audience grew, we knew it was time to be smarter about the content our audience was receiving. There's certainly a longer, learning curve to Infusion Soft, but we are excited about how it has impacted our business just in the short time we've been using it.

Social media automation

I don't believe in automating much, but using a tool like If This Than That (IFTTT) is awesome! I recommend spending an hour looking at what it can do with your different channels, and you'll be glad you did.

Some of my favorite "recipes" include:

- Every Tweet I favorite is saved to a Google Spreadsheet.
- Every Instagram photo I post is saved to a folder in Dropbox.
- Every Instagram photo I post is tweeted as a Twitter image.
- Every time I change my Facebook profile photo, my Twitter profile photo gets updated too.

Social media contests

Running a social-media contest is a great way to grow likes, followers and connections. And when done right, they can give you a nice boost in engagement with your community. A few of my favorite tools are:

- **GroSocial.com.** This tool allows you to create Facebook social promotions and contests, including social photo-contests, giveaways, video contests, viral vote promotions, and newsletter-signup forms.

- **TagBoard.com.** Perfect for events, this lets you search any hashtag, by putting the information you need just a few clicks away.
- **ShortStack.com.** This tool help you create marketing campaigns for free. It positions itself as a marketing hub for social media.

Social media management

There are some great tools out there that can assist with social media management, including scheduling, monitoring mentions and getting more intentional about how you connect with your audience. As I said above, I don't believe in automating everything when it comes to social, but our firm and our clients use some of these to grow and manage social media accounts when appropriate.

- **MeetEdgar.com**

    Edgar is a relatively new tool in the social-media-management world and is the brainchild of Laura Roeder, who was one of the first, social media and online marketers I followed.

    We love Edgar because it provides an easy way to drip out older, but still relevant, content into our social-media streams. Let me give you an example. I have been blogging and creating content like webinars, videos, blog posts, and more for more than three years on my site alone.

    A lot of that content was relevant when it was written, and much of it is still relevant today. The challenge most people have is remembering to re-share a post three, six, or twelve months downs the line.

    Most content gets shared once on Facebook, maybe on Twitter, Instagram, or other networks, and that's it. Edgar allows you to put your content into "buckets." These are things like blog posts, quotes, videos, etc., and then you choose how this content gets dripped out. We use Edgar primarily for Twitter, and it allows older content to be recirculated easily. We also love it for scheduling posts and staying consistent with our Facebook Groups we run and manage.

- **HootSuite**

  I have been a HootSuite fan for years. I fell in love with HootSuite many years ago and still think it's one of the best tools for Twitter. We use it to schedule content, monitor mentions, keyword searches, analytics, and hashtags, and much more. We also love the Team function when working with clients. It allows us access to their social-media accounts without having to pass passwords back and forth. I also am a big fan of the HootSuite app!

- **Facebook Pages Manager mobile app**

  If you have a Facebook Business Page, having the Pages app is a must. The app will allow you to post directly to your Page, schedule content, go live using Facebook Live, upload videos, and boost posts. And, there is a limited view of your Facebook Insights available. I make sure to have our notifications on so I receive a push notification when someone messages me, or our team, on our Page so we can respond quickly. I prefer and recommend using Facebook apps to schedule Facebook Pages content versus using a third-party platform.

Video

- **Animoto.** Animoto is a web-based tool and mobile app that you can use to easily create stunning videos. Animoto was one of the first video-tools I encountered back in 2010, and they have significantly improved it over the years to make it better and better. It still a great place to make a quick, promotional video or educational video, especially if you are on a very limited budget (or no budget!) You simply add photos and text, drop them in the order you'd like them to appear, pick a theme, pick music, and voilà! You have a great looking video.

- **Instagram.** Instagram video is a great place to start with video if you have never created any video before. With up to 60 seconds, it allows you to create short snippets of video content. I see the biggest return on investment in Instagram video when you can create content native to Instagram. For example, I started creating quick videos using nothing more than my iPhone and a tri-pod. And, each video was a quick tip about how to use Instagram. Because these videos were native to Instagram and were made specifically for Instagram (not just something I copied from Facebook), it's no surprise that that type of content does really well.

With this in mind, you can create weekly Instagram videos about your business or industry with one, "quick tip." I can see huge rewards for anyone who does this in service industries, small business owners, real estate professionals, online marketers, and more.

With the addition of Instagram Stories and Instagram Live in 2016 – the possibilities for unique storytelling are endless!

- **Native video in Facebook.** Trying to get more likes, engagement and clicks to your website but feel like your Facebook content is lacking? Try creating video and upload it directly to Facebook. Native video within Facebook, especially if there is text over the video, performs extremely well! You can even create your own video about your business for free using a tool from Facebook at yourbusinessstory. fb.com

- **YouTube.** YouTube has its own editor and for simple editing and annotations, this can be a great solution. You can upload video directly from your mobile phone if needed. Don't forget to always include a title and description in your videos as this helps tremendously with SEO!

- **Periscope.** As of the publishing of this book, Periscope is one of the top, live-video apps you can have on your mobile devices. Owned by Twitter, Periscope allows anyone with a smartphone to live broadcast and engage with the community at large. We are already seeing live video as a game-changer for so many different industries from media, brick-and-mortar businesses, musicians, online marketers, direct-selling companies, business coaches, and more!

Content curation

Curating and finding great content is important to build your credibility and build your brand on social media.

Here are some of my favorite places to curate awesome content:

- **Twitter Lists.** Go to Twitter.com/Lists to create public or private lists on Twitter. To date, this is still one of my favorite tools for finding and curating great content. For example, I have a social-media list that includes some of my favorite bloggers and podcasters on social media. So when I am looking for inspiration, or looking for the latest and greatest, I can simply connect with others in my industry as well as share great content by using Twitter lists.

- **BuzzSumo.com**. Do you need to find a hot, online topic or what your competitors are talking about? BuzzSumo is a fantastic tool to curate great content and get some real-time data on what people are reading and sharing in your industry.

Cloud storage

You have to have a solution to store your photos, videos and social-media calendar in an easily accessible place. We use Dropbox and Google Drive. And, although there are many solutions in this space, we love their ease-of-use. No more emailing photos to one another or sending Word documents back and forth. Everyone has access to Dropbox and Google Drive from any device so it makes our time much more efficient.

Social intelligence

Getting ready for the big, client meeting? We love using CharlieApp.com for insight on our clients, where they were featured in the news recently, their latest social-media posts and more. This helps tremendously with content on any appointment!

We also love SocialMention.com and Mention.net for reputation management on social media. Google Alerts don't always notify you of social-media mentions so both these tools are extremely helpful.

For a complete list of our additional resources, please visit http://katielance.com/resources. After reviewing these resources, it's time to look at creating your social-media policy...

Chapter 22

●　　●　　●

How to Create a Social-Media Policy

Social media is here to stay, so instead of turning your back, embrace the emerging technology by creating a company-wide, social-media policy.

Want to know how to do this? Here are some simple steps to get started...

1. Purpose.

First, get clear on the purpose of your organization and its individual needs. What risks – legal and otherwise – are involved? Part of this endeavor is involving your staff in the decision-making process. Risk is best managed as a team. Bring together everyone in your organization who is directly affected by social media as well as top decision-makers, C-level executives, IT directors and a social-media-savvy attorney too.

2. Core values.

Another consideration is your company's unique set of core values. Every firm is different when it comes to its own set of priorities so this is where you figure out how your social media fits into your company's overall policies, procedures, pending plans, and more. For example, a service-oriented firm that prioritizes responsiveness will want to emphasize this in their social-media-policy draft.

3. Legal ramifications.

Legal ramifications are huge when it comes to the intersection of company and social-media. The National Labor Relations Act protects the employees' right to organize and that includes discussing work conditions over social media. Because of this, it's important to be very careful when it comes to language, dictating what employees can and cannot say on their own social-media platforms.

In this vein, you might want to consider creating dual social-media-policies, one dictating guidelines for employees while at work and the other offering suggestions for employees on their off-hours. Again, you're going to want to be very careful when dealing with the latter.

And when creating guidelines for addressing personal Internet use, you'll want to define acceptable activity inside the office and decide whether employees must disclose their affiliation with your firm when posting information about it.

4. Do your due diligence.

Do your due diligence and research the plethora of federal, labor laws that may be applicable to your social-media policy. For example, the Federal Trade Commission lists its rules on providing disclosures for situations including reviews and endorsements where there is a monetary exchange for social nods.

Additionally, the National Conference of State Legislatures, www.ncsl. org/, breaks down the actions being taken by each state with regard to such laws. Your legal department is also an invaluable resource in terms of advising you how to proceed.

5. Eliminate ambiguity.

When you create your social-media policy, eliminate any ambiguity in regard to roles and responsibilities. Who will be the Facebook whiz? What about the Twitter maven? Delineate these jobs early on so that people have no confusion about who is expected to do what, how and when.

What's next?

Once your policy is complete, take the time to train employees on what it contains. Now is the time to make your new social-media policy both relevant and engaging, while understanding that it will likely spur spirited debate. And that's more than okay – it's encouraged. Get your employees involved and interacting with the new policy, and you'll find that it will enliven it in a new way.

Keep in mind that merely creating the policy is just the tip of the iceberg.

It's going to need to be reviewed for accuracy and relevance at least once every six months. By keeping the framework current, you'll ensure that your social-media efforts have an informative and engaging foundation from which to grow.

Next steps...

Congratulations! Your social-media policy in place, and you're ready to go. All you need to do now is think about the content you want to create to tell the story of what you do and who you are. And remember, content is not a template, and it's not canned. It's authentic, and it's you!

Then, you simply plan your social-media content in a calendar, start posting and see what happens! Please let me know how it goes and share your experiences with me. I'd love to hear from you.

Chapter 23

● ● ●

What's Next?

Congratulations! You have finished this book and are now on the path to being Social Smart! When done correctly, you'll have a successful, social-media platform that allows you to meet new people, build relationships, increase sales… and most important, have fun!

They key is to be intentional, have a plan but don't suffer from analysis paralysis. The best time to start is now. And remember, social media is a marathon, not a sprint. What you do now will affect your business today but more importantly down the line.

The world of social-media is constantly changing so I encourage you to visit my site at katielance.com for the latest updates and tips.

Also, I'd love to hear your comments, insights and feedback about this book. Send me at tweet @katielance or post a comment on our Facebook Page at facebook.com/katielanceconsulting or in our Facebook Group: facebook.com/groups/GetSocialSmartWithKLC. If you are looking for more social media education, we'd love for you to check out our #GetSocialSmart Academy. You can find out more at getsocialsmart.com.

In the meantime, I wish you all the best and will talk to you online soon!

Case Studies
CASE STUDY #1
Social Media Helps to Increase Sales by $1 Million for Real Estate Company

About Coldwell Banker Premier Properties

Coldwell Banker Premier Properties/Premier Homes is an award-winning, full-service real estate company, serving Virginia, West Virginia, Maryland, Pennsylvania, and Washington DC. They endeavor to exceed your expectations with a unique and seamless "one-stop shop" real-estate experience, utilizing in-house relocation, concierge, mortgage, commercial, auction, moving and storage, and settlement services departments.

Before working with Katie Lance Consulting

Before working with Katie Lance, Coldwell Banker Premier Properties used Facebook and Google+ for much of their social media. They also used LinkedIn. However, their LinkedIn use was haphazard according to broker Steve DuBrueler. "In the simplest terms, we didn't know what we didn't know," he states. "We thought we were doing a good job, but weren't."

After consulting with Katie, they realized where their efforts were lacking. This was a result of an eye-opening discovery process that she led them through at the beginning.

They did a lot of things for the community that would be great credibility-and-image-boosters, displaying their caring attitude. But, they didn't share these activities with the community at large, or with their network of brokers and agents through their own, internal platforms.

Katie led them in sharing these activities, and it created meaningful conversations, both online and offline.

After working with Katie

Under the consultation and direction of Katie Lance, the company formulated a more structured and effective, social-media strategy, along with a well-defined content plan. This formed a type of "Readers Digest" of company news and information, according to Steve.

By understanding exactly how Coldwell Banker Premier Properties wanted to be perceived in the community and also internally within the company, Katie Lance designed a social media program that was tailored to their needs, as opposed to a cookie-cutter, one-size-fits-all approach.

The company is now using Twitter, Facebook, LinkedIn and Google+ more effectively as social-media platforms. Many of the company's videos are hosted on YouTube and used across various platforms.

Results

According to Steve, Coldwell Banker Premier Properties had about a 120% increase in growth on Facebook within a 90-day period using Katie's strategies. Their Twitter following doubled, with an increase in shares and Tweets.

Steve said that he can personally account for the video strategy being responsible for at least a million dollars in sales.

The company plans to continue with a structured, social-media strategy as a result of Katie's consultation and planning. They are extending it to the individual agents, helping them strengthen their personal platforms. This includes helping the agents develop something akin to a personal, video résumé. That strategy alone has resulted in a significant increase in transactions for several of the agents.

One more benefit of a structured internal, social-media strategy is that the company has developed a feeling of comradery. With agents and brokers scattered in multiple states, it's easy to become disjointed. A closed Facebook group gives the brokers and agents a safe place to discuss and share their business challenges. "It's brought us closer and made us much more unified," says Steve. "It allows everyone to share and work better as a group."

Case Studies
CASE STUDY #2
Custom Real Estate Software Designers Grow Effective, Social Media Presence

About W+R Studios
Founded in 2008, W&R Studios is a privately held Web software company located in Huntington Beach, California. W+R Studios focuses on creating the next generation of Web-based software solutions for the real-estate industry. By providing a "less is more" approach to software design, elegant user-interfaces, and using the latest in agile programming, W+R Studios' software applications are at the same time powerful, yet accessible, to everyone.

Co-founders Dan Woolley and Greg Robertson have over 20 years of experience each in developing and marketing software in the real-estate industry.

Before working with Katie Lance Consulting
When W+R Studios first started using social media, they didn't have a huge, online presence. According to Frances Brittle, director of marketing at W+R Studios, their efforts were sporadic and disorganized. They felt like social media was something they needed to be a part of but weren't quite sure what to do with it and had a basic, Facebook page and Twitter account. With each product they designed, a new page was created. But they didn't use social media for company-branding.

When they realized they needed to share and integrate these various channels to create a better strategy that would help with the company's branding-efforts, they turned to Katie Lance Consulting for assistance.

After working with Katie

When Katie Lance came on board, she helped them focus and organize their overall strategy, and create their blog content first. Social media was then used to bring the content front-and- center to their targeted market.

Besides developing a structured strategy, Katie provided simple tips that made a huge differences. "Some of her small, quick tips were mind-blowing," states Frances. "They made so much sense. Since she helped us set specific goals, we have definitely increased our following."

Instead of winging it like they did prior to working with Katie Lance Consulting, their social-media efforts became more focused. They developed a content strategy and schedule, created more content on a regular basis and posted more consistently.

They even started a "Fun Friday," where the posts had a more entertaining style to them. This increased engagement and feedback, but it also helped with branding. The posts also gave readers resources they could use.

Results

The strategies worked well. Before working with Katie Lance, the W+R Studios Facebook page had fewer than 1,000 likes. Their audience has now grown to over 3,300 likes and continues to increase consistently.

Along with adding more, social-media channels, W+R Studios is planning to track their efforts more effectively. Frances feels that as they connect more of the dots with promo codes and similar devices, they will better understand where their audience comes from and how they, as a software designer, need to interact with them

Case Studies
CASE STUDY #3
Real Estate Company Builds a Social Media Community That Encourages Conversations Worldwide

About RE/MAX:
From a single office that opened in 1973 in Denver, Colorado, RE/MAX has grown into a global real-estate network of franchisee-owned and -operated offices with more than 100,000 Sales Associates.

Those agents constitute the world's most productive, real-estate sales force. Through their efforts, they've made it possible to say that nobody in the world sells more real estate than RE/MAX.

Before working with Katie Lance Consulting
RE/MAX, LLC had used various, social-media outlets for interacting with their consumer and client base. Originally handled by the PR arm of RE/MAX, social media was eventually moved to the marketing team's responsibility. Facebook, Twitter and YouTube were the primary networks used to connect and communicate with brokers, franchisees and potential clients. But there was a major concern about a lack of engagement. Content was being published, but consumer interaction through comments was almost non-existent.

Abby Lee, VP of Media Strategies, understood the benefit of having an outside, third-party consultant come in and evaluate the current, social-media-strategy. An outside consultant would be able to provide unbiased, clear direction for improving social-media communications that would involve everyone in meaningful conversation.

After working with Katie

Under the direction of Katie Lance Consulting, RE/MAX, LLC began developing social-media networks into virtual communities. Their current channels were revamped and newer networks were evaluated.

According to Abby, "Real estate is a relationship business. We've definitely built better relationships between RE/MAX and our membership, and between our agents and their home buyers and sellers."

The information provided through social networks ensures that agents have good, relevant content to share with their clients. This allows the company to be more responsive, something lacking before they contacted Katie Lance.

Results

For RE/MAX, social media has built an online community that brings together stakeholders, agents and consumers from all over the world. It provides a platform that fosters the communication and conversation that is vital to building strong business relationships.

Case Studies

CASE STUDY #4

A Wine Lover's Passion Sparks a Business Idea, a Mobile App and a Marketplace Brand

About Carla McKay and Crushed™

After more than 20 years in business development and sales positions for big corporations and startups, coupled with eight years of toiling on the weekends for a winery in Sonoma, California, Carla McKay made the leap to the wine industry by creating the Drink Chick consulting firm in 2011. In 2012, she created Crushed.com and the Crushed wine app to power social sharing of wine, which launched in iTunes in December 2013.

Carla is a graduate of the Culinary Institute of America, Greystone School of Wine and a Certified Wine Professional. As an avid bicyclist, you may catch sight of Carla toting wine on her

bike to clients and friends throughout the Bay Area.

Before working with Katie Lance Consulting

When Carla started Crushed, she knew she needed a vibrant, social presence. She wanted an effective social-strategy because her business model was based on social sharing. Putting out the word on Facebook that she was looking for a social-media strategist, she connected with Katie Lance.

Carla mentioned that the Crushed social-media strategy started with her and her partner throwing posts up "haphazardly." They targeted what they thought was their ideal market, millennials. However, the people most interested in their brand were actually women in their 30s and 40s. Katie was able to help steer their efforts towards that group, increasing the value of the brand.

Carla's idea for the app was to provide a method for people to share their wine experiences with others in an easy, real-time way. The main strategy for that was to get people to the Crushed website and get them interested in the content there. As a result, the readers would download the social-sharing app.

After working with Katie

Carla hired Katie Lance several months before the app was launched. Katie helped them build a buzz campaign to get people interested in the app before it actually launched. They wanted the excitement and anticipation to build. A launch party was also hosted when the app was released.

After the launch, Katie put together some press releases and other articles to bring more media attention to Crushed™ and the wine-sharing app.

Results

Because of the advance publicity and launch party, the Crushed app was successful from the start. It was downloaded several thousand times during the first few weeks. The press releases brought several thousand more.

One good takeaway from the experience, according to Carla, is that you need to work hard to be successful, even if you have the best app in the world. Until publicized effectively and people discover that it's out there, any app stands little chance of success.

While Katie got the app and company off to a good start, she also trained the staff in the use of social-media marketing. She was able to get them to the point where the strategies she helped design could be carried out in-house.

Crushed now uses Facebook, Twitter, Instagram, Tumblr and their website in conjunction with their app to promote their brand.

Carla feels that Katie was instrumental in taking Crushed from an idea to an awesome brand in the marketplace. The strategies she designed are still being used by the Crushed team to promote and improve their brand.

Case Studies
CASE STUDY #5
Katie Lance Helps a Startup Build Raving Fans Through Social Media

About Cartavi

In late 2009, Glenn Shimkus and Paul Koziarz set out to develop a highly-mobile app that aimed to remove the friction that comes with managing real estate transactions the old way. The company they created was called Cartavi. And its technology provided real estate professionals with an easier and more secure way to manage, share and sign documents digitally from anywhere, anytime, on any device.

Cartavi eventually became the leading, mobile and collaborative digital transaction management solution for real estate professionals in the U.S. and Canada to help them, "streamline the transaction process and improve the home-purchase experience for consumers." And Katie Lance was a key part of their success…

Before working with Katie Lance Consulting

During the early days of the startup, Glenn and Paul focused primarily on building their product and customer base. And as they began to develop business relationships and industry expertise, they realized that social media would be a great way to access their target market and build brand awareness.

Their audience was spending significant time on sites like Facebook, not only socializing, but searching for, and sharing, information about real estate technology. However, as an early-stage business with limited internal resources, developing and executing a social media strategy to effectively promote their business to real estate professionals was a marketing function that they decided to outsource.

They conducted research to find an experienced marketing professional who had both the integrity and expertise to help them develop a social media strategy that aligned with their brand. After recognizing Katie Lance as a key influencer in social media within the real estate industry, hearing her speak and meeting her at several networking events, they formed a partnership with Katie as a consultant in 2012.

Prior to partnering with Katie Lance Consulting, Cartavi's social media presence was basically managed through a Facebook business page and Twitter handle but lacked the interaction and following that the company desired. But with Katie now on board, that was about to change.

After working with Katie

Katie started the process by conducting a full audit of Cartavi's social media reach and presence. This gave the team a better sense of their current situation and the best way to move forward. Then, they created a plan relative to the type of content they wanted to share (when, where, and how) and put their social media strategy to work.

The Cartavi team began posting more relevant information, and responding to comments, feedback, and support inquiries in real-time. Becoming more present online through social media also allowed the Cartavi Co-founders to engage directly with customers and prospects rather than just posting information. And their audience appreciated their personal approach, accessibility, and the fact that there were real people at Cartavi sharing their story as the company grew. Followers began to increase, and Cartavi soon realized the value of what they were doing, not only from a marketing perspective, but also from the connections they were creating.

"Listening to and collaborating with our customers was essential to building our products, our services, and our brand," said Paul Koziarz, co-founder and former chief marketing officer of Cartavi. "Social media allowed us to further share our story, and gave us a more meaningful way to inspire, inform and interact with real estate professionals."

Building on the success of their new, social media efforts, Katie and Paul decided to develop an online community to better connect their growing family of users and supporters. The community, called "Friends and Family of Cartavi," was a private Facebook group designed specifically for an increasing number of real estate professionals who were interested in, or already using, their products.

The creation of the Facebook group opened the door to real conversations where people openly talked about the product and shared their input with the Cartavi team as well as other members. Over time, several product enhancements were developed in response to the feedback that was being shared through the online conversations. And as the community grew, several, highly-active members became evangelists or "ambassadors" who enthusiastically helped promote the brand.

"While we didn't set out to develop an ambassador program at the time, that is basically what happened as a result of becoming more engaged with our customers and followers through social media," said Koziarz "We were very fortunate to earn the trust and support of so many great real estate professionals who believed in what we were doing and who were more than willing to share their Cartavi experience with others."

Results

Through the partnership with Katie Lance Consulting, Cartavi learned how to better leverage social media to improve their product by engaging with their audience and grow their brand by turning followers into raving fans. Their marketing campaigns reached record levels and generated conversations that got real estate professionals talking about the brand online. In fact, Paul estimates that their Facebook following grew from a few hundred to nearly 5,000 in a matter of months while working with Katie Lance.

Katie played a vital role in helping Cartavi develop it's social media strategy and improve audience engagement. Her expertise and deep knowledge of the real estate industry proved to be invaluable as Cartavi reached a significant milestone as a company.

In May 2013, Cartavi was acquired by DocuSign, the global standard for eSignature and digital transaction management. The acquisition followed an 18-month strategic partnership, during which the companies jointly developed solutions for the real estate industry. Through the merger, Cartavi became part of the DocuSign brand. And as the company and its products were being integrated into DocuSign's system, so were the social media programs and communities that Cartavi had created. Katie provided continued support to Cartavi throughout the integration process and worked with DocuSign's internal marketing team to help make the transition as seamless as possible for Cartavi's customers and followers online.

"Katie Lance is one of the most well-recognized and respected marketing professionals in the real estate industry. Her passion for social media and technology, and her vast experience in helping businesses grow their brands are evident from the moment you meet her," states Koziarz. "It was a pleasure working with Katie, and I would highly recommend her to anyone in need of a trusted social media expert."

Case Studies
CASE STUDY #6
Mortgage Company Increases Their Online Presence and Thought Leadership with an Effective Social-Media Strategy

About RPM Mortgage, Inc.
In 1995, Rob and Tracey Hirt asked one another "what if...?" and were inspired to create a mortgage business where the loan advisors were the primary customer and sales and marketing laid the foundation for success. It was a concept unlike any other.

The result of their vision and hard work was RPM Mortgage, Inc., an independently-owned and operated residential mortgage-lending company with more than 650 loan advisors and employees who have been enabled to provide better results for their customers.

Before working with Katie Lance Consulting

RPM's social-media presence was "anemic," according to Jill Sonderby, SVP of Marketing and Communications. They knew they needed a social-media presence but had no actual strategy to implement it.

According to Jill, "someone set up our profiles for Facebook, Twitter and LinkedIn, but never did much with them. As a result, they were very quiet with no real interaction going on with anyone."

To change that, they hired Katie Lance Consulting to help them improve their social presence by creating an effective social-media strategy.

After working with Katie

With Katie onboard, RPM developed a social-media strategy to increase their exposure to the different audiences with whom they needed to interact.

In the beginning, Katie was not just a consultant – she managed the content and executed much of the social-media content publishing. With Katie Lance's help, Jill made quality decisions about what kind of content was needed and who it should target.

Katie also helped RPM's loan advisors set up their individual profiles and provided tips and advice to make their profiles more effective. Additionally, she held webinars and advised them on the best technology solutions for their programs.

As their collaboration progressed, Jill stated that there was a need to hire in-house staff to handle the expanding, social-media strategy. Katie worked with her to develop a job description and assisted in the in-house staff training.

Under Katie's guidance, RPM was able to expand their social-media efforts to include social-media platforms that would help support the loan advisors that worked within the company.

Results

As a result of Katie's planning and training, RPM was able to meet several of their goals. First, they expanded their presence in front of their targeted market and let them see what mortgage solutions they had to offer.

They were also able to do a better job of recruiting loan advisors, particularly those with a more professional LinkedIn presence.

When it was necessary to ensure compliance with the marketing and advertising standards, Katie's knowledge of the industry helped. Both the company and the loan advisors were protected because they used the platforms and content that ensured compliance.

Some of the benefits that RPM gained under Katie Lance's guidance were:

- Better search results without having to pay for Google AdWords and other paid search-programs.
- Improved relationships with real-estate professionals who worked with the company's mortgage professionals.
- More exposure online and via mobile using the social-media solutions Katie helped build.

A company blog was also developed to increase their online presence. The blog includes content written by company personnel and industry leaders. This helps promotes RPM as a thought leader in the mortgage business.

Katie's ability to view the project from both the company's and the customer's perspective provided a balanced understanding of what was necessary to improve RPM's social presence in the marketplace.

Additional Resources

Here are some additional resources that may be helpful to you in your social media journey!

Free Downloads:

- Content Grid: http://katielance.com/contentgrid
- Facebook Live Cheat-Sheet: http://katielance.com/facebooklivedownload

Katie Lance's blog: http://www.katielance.com/blog

Connect with Katie Lance on Social Media:

- https://www.facebook.com/KatieLanceConsulting/
- https://www.facebook.com/groups/GetSocialSmartWithKLC/
- https://twitter.com/katielance
- https://www.linkedin.com/in/katielance
- https://www.instagram.com/katielance/
- https://www.youtube.com/user/KatieLanceConsulting/

- https://www.periscope.tv/katielance
- https://www.pinterest.com/katielance1/
- https://www.snapchat.com/add/katielance1

Looking to take your social media strategy to the next level? Join our online #GetSocialSmart Academy here: http://getsocialsmart.com/

Acknowledgements

This book has been more than a year in the making and really more than a decade has passed since I first thought to myself, "I think I'd like to write a book." Little did I know the amount of time and effort it takes to create and write a book!

There are many people to thank who have supported and loved me along the way. A big thank you to my husband and partner in life and in business. Paul, you are my best friend and your love and support has meant the world to me.

To my boys Owen and Luke: You are my reason 'why' each and every day. I love you to the moon and back!

To my parents, Jack and Shelley Graham, my brother and sister-in-law, Mike and Kathleen Graham and my amazing extended family – I love you all more than words can say and am so thankful for your love and support.

To my grandparents in heaven, I miss your tenacity, your wit and your laughter. This book is dedicated to your legacy.

To my incredible team – there really aren't enough words to thank you for your hard work, your hustle and how hard you work behind-the-scenes to make what we do look seamless. I feel so honored to work with you everyday: Melissa, Megan, Ann Marie, Jenn and Paul – thank you!

To my clients - thank you for trusting me to work with you and a special thank you to all the amazing people and companies that contributed to the case study portion of this book.

To my friends all over the country - thank you for giving me a platform to share my passion and my message, and for your support and your friendship. It means the world!

A big thank you to Kim Garst for writing the forward for this book and for being a great mentor to me!

Finally, a big thank you to my editor and writing partner Melanie Rembrandt – thank you for all of your insight, your patience and for walking down this path with me. It is so appreciated.

About the Author

Katie is the CEO and Owner of Katie Lance Consulting – a social media marketing firm. With more than fifteen years of marketing and branding experience, Katie specializes in working with companies to help develop and implement their social media and content strategy. Katie's client roster include includes companies such as RE/MAX International, DocuSign, Realtor.com, SmartZip, Mason-McDuffie Mortgage and many others. Since 2012, Katie's firm has worked closely with hundreds of companies in the real estate, technology, mortgage and start-up space.

Katie is a nationally known and highly sought-after keynote speaker at conferences across the globe; teaching the latest tools and strategies in social media, mobile and technology trends.

Her signature group social media program; the #GetSocialSmart Academy has received accolades from industry peers across the globe.

Katie is a passionate writer and is a frequent contributor to The Huffington Post, Social Media Examiner and Women 2.0. She is passionate about all things tech, wine and empowering women in leadership.

Formerly, Katie was the Chief Strategist for Inman News and has been listed by Inman as one of the top 100 influential people in real estate. She has also been listed in the Swanepoel Trends Report as one of the 20 most powerful social media professionals in real estate.

Katie lives in the San Francisco Bay Area with her husband and 2 beautiful boys.